BOOK OF THE
MONGREL

The Authors

Kay White, MIACE, writes regularly for many canine magazines, including the *Veterinary Times, Kennel Gazette* and *Dog World*. She has written and co-written fourteen books about dogs and cats, and has pioneered the provision of educational facilities for dog owners and breeders. She attends and reports on the major veterinary conferences and meetings on animal behaviour, and used to own boarding and breeding kennels in Surrey, England. Kay White now lives in Sussex with her husband and four dogs.

Andrew Prentis BVSc, MRCVS, is Director of the Beaumont Animals' Hospital, a teaching hospital of the Royal Veterinary College, London. He has also worked as Veterinary Technical Director of the Society for the Protection of Animals in North Africa, and from 1986-1991 he was Veterinary Director of the RSPCA's Southern Hospital Group.

BOOK OF THE
MONGREL

HarperCollins*Publishers*

KAY WHITE MIACE
HEALTHCARE: ANDREW PRENTIS BVSC, MRCVS

First published in 1997 by
HarperCollins*Publishers*, London

02 01 00 99 98 97

9 8 7 6 5 4 3 2 1

A catalogue record of this book is available from the British Library

ISBN 0 00 413307 2

This book was created by SP Creative Design for HarperCollins*Publishers* Ltd
Editor: Heather Thomas
Designer: Rolando Ugolini
Artwork: Al Rockall and Rolando Ugolini

Photography by David Dalton and Rolando Ugolini

Acknowledgements
The publishers would like to thank the following for their kind assistance in producing this book: Scampers School for Dogs for their help with photography, and special thanks to Charlie Clarricoates for all his hard work and his dogs Timmy and Gemma. Luan Brame and her dog Simba; Lorna Evans and her dog Duke; Karen Lyons and her dogs Lenny and Boyce; Amanda Cox and Brandy; Sarah Carmichael and Floozie; Sharon Wing and Legend; Wendy Jones and Bubbles and Chuck; Samantha Luck and Baloo; and Michelle Wilson and Edward. Our thanks also to Mrs Phipps at Bretlyn Kennels and Polly, Diva, Shadow and Bunty.

The RSPCA is a registered charity and HarperCollins*Publishers* is paying 2½% of the recommended retail price of £9.99 to the RSPCA.

Colour reproduction by Colourscan, Singapore
Printed and bound by New Interlitho, SpA, Milan, Italy

CONTENTS

FOREWORD

The RSPCA is delighted to have been involved in the production of this book, which is truly unique in its focus on the mongrel dog. Every year the RSPCA rehomes over 29,000 dogs which have been abandoned or, for some reason, are unwanted by their owners. Sadly, most of these are dogs of mixed origins – mongrels. And yet mongrels can make the most delightful pets. They can show the characteristics of every and any breed and sometimes of no known breeds at all! In health terms they can score more highly than the pure-breds since their hybrid vigour guards them from the genetic abnormalities that can result from selective breeding.

This book is essential reading for any existing or would-be mongrel dog owner. It tells you what makes your pet tick, so that you can create the best environment for a fit and happy dog. Only by understanding your dog's behaviour and needs can you be sure of looking after it properly and giving it the kind of life it deserves.

Bill Swann
Head of RSPCA Veterinary Department

NF029344

WHAT ARE MONGRELS?

Let's begin by saying that it is not an insult to call a dog a mongrel. The word is derived from the now obsolete Middle English word *Meng* (to mix) or the Old English *Gemong* (a mingling). A mongrel is a dog of random breeding, in contrast with what we term pedigree dogs, which may have been bred selectively for many thousands of years, whether or not the parents actually had a recorded pedigree.

Early Egyptian paintings of dogs, *circa* 4,000 B.C., show hounds not unlike the Greyhounds and Whippets that we know today. These early dogs, which are now generally agreed to be domesticated individuals from the smaller wolf strains, had no written pedigree, but they were bred like to like in looks and also in speed and hunting ability, i.e. they were selected for and developed to use their natural attributes for the benefit of man. At the other end of the ancient canine size scale is the Pekingese, known and treasured as 'under the table dogs' by the Emperor and court of the Han Dynasty in China, around 200 B.C. Pekingese were not working dogs; on the contrary, they were kept solely for the pleasure they gave and as objects of beauty.

As the early nomadic tribes settled and engaged in agricultural work as a way of life, dogs that could herd livestock and also guard them from wolves and other predators became important. In Britain in the Middle Ages, dogs were a very important part of the sporting passions of the day: bull-baiting and stag hunting.

SELECTIVE BREEDING

Dogs have been selectively bred down the ages to hunt game, to chase and catch, to retrieve, to scent, to go to ground after vermin and also to guard man and his property against intruders.

Each type of dog was developed with the physique and physical conformation best suited to his appointed work. A dog's speed and willingness to work was an attribute for the owner to boast about and, consequently, family lines of dogs

Above: mongrels with terrier ancestry often have shaggy or wiry coats and a strong independent streak.

which had a standard of excellence were in demand. From these family lines the concept of recorded pedigrees developed but this was many years after recognisable breeds of dogs were known and used. For example, Foxhound pedigree recording began in 1787.

However, if you should ever be made to feel that your mongrel lacks a pedigree written down for all to see, perhaps it may be a comfort to remember that there is no positive proof to link any dog to its recorded pedigree. And if you want to boast about the antiquity of your own mongrel's line, you may be interested to know that one of the oldest dog skeletons found in Britain, at Avebury in Wiltshire, and thought to date from before 3,000 B.C., was a domestic (mongrel) dog. It was long-legged, short-backed and small-headed with a skull shorter than that of a hound. It was therefore not a specialized dog, and not intended for hunting, herding or guarding – just a dog, which archaeologists identified as a kind of ancient British pariah dog.

The word 'pariah' is an Indian one, and is applied to feral dogs that live in and around villages but which are not owned by any one person. These mongrels have a reputation for being of good temperament and for a willingness to follow anyone who appears to be doing anything remotely interesting. Feral mongrels usually have no territory or possessions of their own and so are spared the need to guard or to show hostility to people who approach them.

As the writer Hugh Walpole described his own dog in the *Jeremy and Hamlet* stories written in the 1930s:

'I have owned a great many dogs, some of them very finely bred, very aristocratic, very intelligent but none of them has ever approached Hamlet for wisdom, conceit, self-reliance and true affection.

'He was a ghastly mongrel, I tremble to think of the many different breeds of dogs that have gone into his making, but he had Character, he had Heart, he had an unconquerable zest for life.'

Does that not sum up all the mongrels we know?

RANDOMLY-BRED DOGS

Mongrels are truly randomly bred, hardly ever asking their owner's permission for the coupling and never requiring any persuasion to mate as some of the more inhibited pedigree breeds do.

The mongrel may well be the product of many generations of chance matings; no wonder some people call them 'Heinz 57s', reflecting the famous advertisements for that company's fifty-seven product lines. Others call them 'curs' but this is an unkind term, originally referring to a vicious mongrel, and shortened from the thirteenth-century word *Kurdogge* and the old Norse word for 'growl'. Another term, which has fallen into disuse, is the Yorkshire expression, a 'tyke', meaning a rough-coated, shaggy mongrel. Some people call mongrels 'mutts' but that word has overtones of stupidity and mongrels are usually very bright and quick to learn. Perhaps the slang term 'bitzer' suits your mongrel best of all?

Nearly everyone likes to speculate on the breeds that created their own bitzer, but in fact this is only really possible in cross-breeds. True mongrels have more ingredients than a Christmas Pudding and it is almost impossible to know which of their assortment of genes will dominate their looks. They have infinite and unpredictable variety. Even when two similar mongrels are mated together, it is very possible that none of the offspring will resemble in colour and markings either of their parents.

Mongrel genes are like the pretty pieces of glass in a kaleidoscope; shake them up and a totally different design results every time.

SIZE

One of the frequently quoted drawbacks in taking on a mongrel puppy is that you can't predict how big he will grow, but true mongrels are rarely extreme in size. They are most frequently average in size, with a height range of between 38-41 cm (15-16 in) minimum and 54-57 cm (22-23 in) maximum.

However, it is important that we learn to differentiate between mongrels and cross-breeds. Little dogs, such as Yorkshire Terriers, Papillons and the smaller Spitz breeds, are sometimes mated together, either by design or accident, and these cross-breeds are likely to be small.

THE WAY MONGRELS LOOK

Mongrels are generally medium-sized dogs and their muzzles are, almost without exception, pointed. The broad-muzzled, flat-faced type of dog, as seen in Boxers and Pugs, rarely survives even the first crossing.

◆ **Ears** may be pricked up, and open, ready to catch every sound; or they may be folded over or set on the side of the face and hanging down; or the dog may have one of each kind. The ears may be set high on the head, or down at eye level. On-top ears are the most flexible kind: one or both may be cocked up to demonstrate their alertness, or they may be flexed backwards and flattened to indicate fear or guilt. Some ears may be fringed and drooping, sometimes with an attractive hairdresser-style flick-up at the tips. One ear held higher than the other may indicate a painful ear problem, or it may be just the way your mongrel likes to carry them. The great thing about mongrels is that they and their owners see no reason to conform to any preconceived designs.

◆ **Tails** have infinite variety too. They may be wonderfully plumed and feathered and curled over the back like a teapot handle, or held out behind like a fox's brush. On a smooth-coated mongrel the tail also may be smooth and thick like a mooring rope, held aloft like a signalling flag or carried down as a rudder. But, just for fun, a smooth-coated dog may sport a feathered plume.

◆ **Coats** can be of any texture, quite

Left and opposite: mongrels come in all coat textures, colours, sizes and temperaments. The infinite variety all adds to the fun and joy of owning these independent and spirited dogs.

DOCKING

There is never any case for trying to get a mongrel's or a cross-breed's tail docked. The tail is a very important communication aid, especially when indicating their friendly intentions to other dogs, so never attempt to deprive the dog of this valuable and vital asset.

smooth with densely-packed short hairs, or with slightly longer and silky hair, or really long and shaggy all over, about 12.5-15 cm (5-6 in) long. Some dogs have stiff wire hair and bristly whiskers on the muzzle. Dense wire-haired coats may need professional stripping at least once a year, and although this is an expense, your mongrel will appreciate having the dead hair removed, and he will look very much smarter.

◆ **Eyes** may be round and dark, or oval: the colour range is from bluish grey, through amber and yellow to very dark brown.

◆ **The nose** almost invariably ends in a very wet black blob. Mongrels rarely have to put up with the pinkish and greyish seasonal change in nose colour which affects some pedigree breeds.

◆ **Coat colour** is another rainbow story. Tans, brown, black with tan trimmings, all over golden or foxy red, white with black patches, black with white shirt-front, black with white ticking, white with red saddle and ears, white with irregular red or brown patches, each in its own way attractive. More unusual is the black-and-tan

brindle effect coat, set off by touches of white. Alas, the most commonly seen mongrel wears a medium-length solid black coat grown at random length, accompanied by a smart white shirt-front, but this is the mongrel most frequently passed over, when people go to choose a pet from a rescue kennel.

Above: this mischievous little dog has clearly identifiable Westie ancestry.

◆ Mongrels that live in kind considerate homes and have been adopted early in their lives are of middle-weight athletic build with straight front legs and well-muscled hind legs especially suited to high jumping. Mongrels that have had a hard time in their youth may never quite achieve the hard, conditioned body and luxuriant coat that they might have had.

◆ The mongrel's talent shows through in the way in which they recover their trust in humans even when they have endured very bad treatment which they have done nothing to deserve.

Left: most mongrels are fun-loving and intelligent dogs who need a lot of stimulating games and exercise.

CROSS-BREEDS

These are the result of mating two different breeds together. Such matings may arise by accident, when two different breeds are kept in one household or in one kennel compound. Sometimes a cross-breeding is deliberately undertaken to introduce features lacking in a pure-bred dog. If this is a planned outcrossing of a pedigree line the strategy has to be presented and explained to the Kennel Club and permission to make the cross obtained before the mating takes place. You cannot register the resulting puppies, but if the next three generations descending from cross-breds are mated back into their own breed, it is possible that the Kennel Club may accept the fourth generation for

Below: this Border Collie cross-bred dog may be the result of a deliberate or an accidental mating.

> Left: German Shepherd influence is clearly evident in this dog's head shape and ear carriage.

resultant litter was unlike either of the parents, but when the pups were, in time, back-crossed to a Cocker, or to a Basenji, traces of the ancestral features were shown.

The most famous cross-breds of our time are probably Queen Elizabeth's Dorgis, an accidental litter resulting from a mating between a Dachshund and a Corgi. A painting of the Queen surrounded by her Corgis and a Dorgi hangs in The Kennel Club, casting a bright eye over all the pure-breds that are registered there.

IDENTIFYING ANCESTRY

Cross-bred ancestry in the first generation of the cross can be picked out fairly easily: German Shepherd Dog influence comes through very strongly in head shape and ear carriage; Springer Spaniels pass on their

registration as pure-bred. It is, in fact, surprising how some trait echoing another breed will show up, possibly in only one puppy in a litter, perhaps many generations down the family tree.

Scott and Fuller, the geneticists and animal behaviourists who studied a large population of dogs in an American experimental laboratory in 1965, mated together Basenjis and Cocker Spaniels. The

GUIDE DOGS

The Guide Dogs for the Blind Association have created one of the most useful crosses in mating Labradors to Golden Retrievers, to attempt to blend the best attributes of both breeds. The resulting litters have proved to have an extremely high success rate as dogs for guiding blind people: the willingness to co-operate with the owner, shown by the Labrador, has blended well with the instinctive liveliness and agility of the Golden Retriever. However, this cross is made once only, and the cross-breds are not bred back to each other.

KENNEL CLUB REGISTRATION

The U.K. Kennel Club regulations about registration state that no dog shall be entered on any breed register unless each of its parents is entered in that register. Imported dogs of new breeds go onto a special register, but only if they have come from a country where there is a recognised canine Stud Book. Dogs of any ancestry may be entered in the Obedience and Working Trials Register, but they must not be entered in any form of competition under the Kennel Club's jurisdiction except for Obedience Classes, Working Trials and Agility Tests. The progeny of such dogs may be registered only in this register.

colouring and markings, as do the Border Collies. Black colouring will often dominate all other colours. Mixing dogs that have a very distinctive hair coat can bring about problems later in life: for instance, a Labrador crossed with an Old English Sheepdog may retain the Labrador's double undercoat but may grow a long Old English Sheepdog coat on top of it. The shedding problems and the overheating may create their own difficulties for the owner.

Character traits may not blend well either – a cross between a Dobermann and a Jack Russell may create an extremely sharp little dog whose bite may well be as bad as its bark. The keep-on-running attributes of a Saluki, crossed with the riot-raising potential of a Border Collie, will also not make an easy-to-live-with dog. A cross that appears to be most successful is that of a Yorkshire Terrier with a Maltese Terrier. These dogs may be larger than the average Yorkie, but sport a 'bad hair day'

kind of coat of a rough texture in silver and gold colouring.

When writing of cross-breeds, it may be useful to point out that if a pedigree bitch has a litter by a dog that is not of her own breed, there is no truth in the belief that all future litters will be tainted in some way. Mated to an individual in her

JACK RUSSELLS

These very popular little terriers make lively and interesting pets. They are not pure-bred, but then neither are they mongrels. Their colouring is mainly white with tan or red patches, and the coat may be wire-haired or smooth, both varieties thereby betraying their Fox Terrier ancestry.

Jack Russells are not recognised at Kennel Club Shows, nor are they permitted to be registered at the Kennel Club. Comparatively recently, the Kennel Club has recognised the Parson Jack Russell Terrier, a taller-on-the-leg Fox Terrier, similar to the favourites of Edwardian days. This terrier is reminiscent of the type said to have been bred in the early nineteenth century by the Reverend John Russell, after whom the breed is named.

own breed, the bitch should have a pure-bred litter which can be registered at the Kennel Club.

But to breed a cross-bred to another cross-bred is to lose many of the original attributes and those who do so may be well on the way to creating a mongrel.

HEALTH

Mongrels are popularly supposed to be more healthy than pure-bred dogs, and this may well be true, given that the close in-breeding of some pedigree dogs tends to concentrate the genes that produce hereditary diseases, such as hip dysplasia, some heart defects, abnormalities of the eyes, and skin problems. Not every pure-bred dog suffers from these diseases, but a considerable number do.

However, the random-bred dog does not carry such an intensity of inherited characteristics, although mongrels are just as susceptible to all the infectious diseases, such as distemper and its complications, leptospirosis, hepatitis, canine parvovirus and infectious tracheo-bronchitis, familiarly known as kennel cough. Mongrels are just as susceptible to internal and external parasites, to digestive problems and chronic diarrhoea, to kidney problems, obstructions of the throat and gut, and food poisoning through scavenging. So mongrels are by no means exempt from veterinary expenses.

Cross-breeds, unless intentionally and carefully planned, may come with

Above: free-spirited mongrels love to run off the lead. If possible, let your dog run free in a safe place every day.

the hereditary diseases of both their parents, and those further back in their pedigree. Mongrels do tend to live longer than pedigree dogs; they have an in-built determination to survive.

TEMPERAMENT AND ATTRIBUTES

Most mongrel addicts will agree that no matter what their dog's ancestry, he has inherited agility, cleverness and the ability to learn quickly and to continue to apply what he has learnt, plus abundant vigour to join in whatever his human family wants to do.

ANTISOCIAL BEHAVIOUR

Possibly the worst trait that the mongrel has inherited is the over-riding passion for running free, for wandering, and for scavenging. Some fifty years ago this mongrel behaviour was tolerated, but it is not acceptable nowadays. However difficult it may seem, mongrels must be confined within their owner's premises. There is no special dispensation that they may run free.

The worst mongrel sin of all is that of hanging around outside houses where bitches in season are kept, and molesting them when they are out for walks with their owners. These traits are not actually the mongrel's fault, but are caused by the anti-social behaviour of mongrel owners. Certainly the mongrel shows no hesitation in taking up the offer of free running and demonstrating the canine version of loutish behaviour, but it is the owner who, ultimately, should be in control of the dog.

It is not justifiable to say that a free-running mongrel has a charming temperament and means no harm when he teases the Rottweiler walking sedately on the lead or when he jumps playfully around the old lady who is concerned about her shopping.

Free-running dogs, whether pure-bred or mongrel, are not socially acceptable. Mongrels can appear to be very clever at crossing the road in perfect safety but they do not always get it right, and some

Below: it is important for dogs to socialize and to meet other dogs, even when on the lead, without behaving aggressively towards each other.

THE DANGEROUS DOGS ACT 1991

The Dangerous Dogs Act 1991 imposed severe restrictions on ownership of specified types of dog (e.g. the American Pit Bull Terrier) which had been bred for fighting purposes. Regulations required compulsory neutering and microchipping for all such dogs which must be muzzled and kept on a lead when in public. The law imposed a mandatory death penalty on the dog for breaches of this law.

The RSPCA supported the original intentions of the Act which placed restrictions on types of dog bred for fighting purposes to protect the public from attack. But it believed that animals should no longer face a mandatory death penalty if their owners broke this law.

The RSPCA strongly supports protecting the public but does not endorse the unnecessary euthanasia of any animal. As a result of intense campaigning by the RSPCA and the general public, the Act was amended in June 1997 so that the courts now have discretionary powers over whether a dog should be destroyed. The courts can also allow the register of exempted dogs to be reopened in cases where owners have legitimate reasons for not having registered their dog.

dogs sustain terrible injuries just because their owners let them run free. Worse still, some multiple vehicle crashes occur because a car swerves to avoid a dog that is running in the road.

If you take pleasure in owning a mongrel, then he must be cared for in just the same way as an expensive pedigree dog. He must not be allowed to chase cars and bicycles, overturn dustbins, bark intolerably, leave faeces on the pavement, pick fights with other dogs, or to run loose in children's playgrounds.

Mongrels must be protected from behaving badly just as vigilantly as the rarest of pedigree specimens. There is no place for badly behaved and anti-social dogs in modern society.

CONTROL

The desire to run free, to perform daring feats of athletic behaviour by jumping into next-door's larder window, to dash across motorways and to track down every bitch in the neighbourhood is buried deeply in the subconscious of every mongrel. After all, that kind of behaviour is what founded the mongrel type.

Dogs used to be tolerated in urban and suburban streets, and disregarded if they ran into shops and stole food. In Georgian and Victorian times, the streets were full of dogs; indeed, the canine population of Britain was estimated to be about 1,000,000 dogs in 1796, but the imposition of a tax on dogs resulted in the killing of hundreds of dogs when the owners would not pay. Thousands of dogs were turned out on to the streets, and bodies piled up at the roadside.

The nineteenth century was a time of widespread cruelty to dogs. Organised dog fights and the baiting of bulls or even wild animals by dogs were popular public spectacles. However, compassion for animals was also stirring. The Society for the Prevention of Cruelty to Animals was founded in 1824, when the future Queen Victoria was a small child. Later in her life she granted the Society the accolade of becoming a Royal Society. Possibly one of the greatest dog cruelties that the RSPCA managed to get abolished was the use of dog teams for transport purposes.

Dogs had been used by tradesmen to carry their packs of tools and equipment ever since the sixteenth century, but it was in the 1800s that dogs became a general means of transport for goods that had to be delivered quickly. Butchers' carts in London were drawn by teams of five dogs, and letters were also carried in dog carts. Dogs were often driven for long distances on hard roads until they fell exhausted, when they would be turned loose, to wander or to die on the streets, and fresh dogs put in their place. The RSPCA worked long and hard petitioning Parliament against this cruelty. Now there is no dog tax, but Britain has around 7,000,000 dogs and, ideally, none should be loose on the streets.

Left: your dog should always be under control. When taking him out for a walk in a public place, put him on a lead.

DECIDING TO ACQUIRE A DOG

You and your family have probably had the same discussion over and over again. You all want a dog, and you have decided you want the pleasure and the challenge of taking on a mongrel or cross-breed. However, before making an irrevocable decision, you have to take a long, honest look at yourself, your immediate family, your lifestyle and your future prospects. 'A Dog is for Life', as the slogan goes, so if you do take on a dog you will be putting yourself, or someone close to you, into the role of a canine foster parent for at least the next ten years. Can you foresee that you will be able to give a dog all that he needs for that time? What if your own life changes? Are you sure there will always be a suitable home, human companionship and affectionate care for the dog for that length of time?

The promise you make when you decide to have a dog or a puppy is increasingly difficult to keep when very few people are able to forecast their future income, job and homes; so the very

best you can do is to say that wherever you go, your dog will go too. Your home, accommodation and your leisure pursuits will also always be chosen with the dog in mind. You cannot divorce a dog; their devotion to their owner is too strong for that. It is true that if you take a puppy or a grown dog from a rescue home, you

assume the role of a foster-owner, and the rescue society usually promises to take the dog back if you cannot keep him. But this is no way to treat a dog: to take him into your home when it suits you and to send him back when he becomes inconvenient. Could you bear to see your dog put back into a compartment in a communal kennel, to wait day after day hoping that you will be next through the door to claim him again – that the banishment has all been a dreadful mistake?

Once you have tamed the dog and made him yours, that is what he is – your dog. You are considering adopting a living creature which will become part of your family, in sickness and in health, in fun and frolics, in deliberate naughtiness and in incredible cleverness, in joy and laughter and in much appreciated comforting companionship.

Right: having enough time to spend with a pet is a crucial factor in deciding to own a dog.

COMPANIONSHIP

Puppies and grown dogs have so much to give us, but what they need is our companionship in return. True, you need space for a dog, and you need money for his keep, insurance and any ancillary expenses, but most of all you need time. There is no pure-bred dog, mongrel or cross-breed who enjoys or even tolerates being left alone for any length of time.

We have to remember that dogs, and the wolves who were their ancestors,

originally lived in packs. Members of the pack are playmates, disciplinarians, decision takers, comforters and teachers for each other. A good attentive owner can fulfil all these roles, but the dog left on his own is a sorry creature; dogs feel loneliness more than any other pets.

Therefore, do not take on a dog if you are likely to have to leave him alone for several hours a day; it just does not work out. This is especially true with mongrels and cross-breds, which may already have experienced a communal life. Two hours a day is as long as any adult dog should be left; and puppies should hardly be left at all, because they cannot learn acceptable behaviour if there is no-one there to teach them. A puppy will never become house-trained unless you are always there to do the training and to remind him of what is wanted.

Dogs are not unlike children. They can be a nuisance at times, and they can curtail our freedom to do exactly as we wish – to come home or to stay away just as the whim takes us. 'I've got to get back to the dog' sounds a bit foolish to non-dog owners, but it is true; you have a duty to fulfil to your animal.

HOME ALONE

When you take on a dog, your house and garden are bound to suffer some minor damage, and at times your dog may be a defiant disobeyer of your rules of conduct.

SHOULD YOU HAVE A DOG?

◆ Are you allowed to have a dog where you live now? A surprising number of desirable living spaces do not allow dogs; enquire first rather than try to argue later.

◆ You have to consider your leisure time. Do you do things at weekends which will allow the dog to join in? For example, sailing, fishing and cycling are not dog-friendly activities unlike walking and dog-orientated training and agility games .

◆ Do not feel that you are denied dog companionship if you have to decide that you do not have enough time to give to a dog; nearly all the rescue societies would be only too glad to have you adopt a dog, to visit him, groom him, even take him for walks and train him in good behaviour.

A mongrel may be particularly difficult to fence in owing to his in-built trait to enjoy running free and to join a pack of canine scavengers and fun-seekers.

One reason why there are fewer mongrels about nowadays is the dramatic increase in motor traffic and increased number of dog wardens, who quickly take wanderers into custody. Your dog, if left alone, may be a target for complaint from

ADULT DOG OR PUPPY?

Do you want an adult dog or a puppy? If you have the time to look after him, a pup must be the best choice. Also, if you already have a dog in your household, a grown dog may be resentful of another adult being imported. However, most dogs will accept and enjoy a puppy. Your adult may help you in training the puppy in house manners and being a comforter to him in the lonely hours of the night.

your neighbours. They may be irritated by barking or they may feel that the dog's howling means he is being cruelly treated. And, to some extent, they may be right, for a dog usually only howls when he is left alone, and that is cruelty to a dog who depends on your company. You, or some other responsible person, must stay with your dog for as long as possible during the day.

LONELINESS
Loneliness is the one most constant factor that breaks down the dog/human relationship. Some people end up disliking their dogs if they tear up the house or soil the floors every time

they go out. However, you should never forget that you are the cause of these behaviour patterns. If you leave the dog alone for long periods of time, you are expecting too much from a very intelligent animal which was not created for a solitary existence. This is especially true if you take an adult dog from a rescue kennel, as being alone will be totally alien to his experience. In kennels there are other dogs in neighbouring pens, there are always kennel workers about and there are even visitors to bring that glow of hope of a real home at last. It is doubtful that any dog visualizes a real home as a custom-built kitchen into which he is shut alone all day.

What every dog requires from you is companionship and, a measure of patience. The capability to be with your dog constantly if you take on a puppy, and not to plan to leave him alone for more than two hours at a stretch when

he is older, is the most crucial factor when deciding whether you should have a dog.

EXPENSE AND RUNNING COSTS

What about costs? Apart from the initial purchase price, the running costs of a mongrel are about the same as for a pedigree dog of the same size.

◆ **FEEDING**

We have come a long way from the time when it was customary to feed a pet dog on household scraps. We know now that to keep a dog in good health he must have a balanced diet of carbohydrates, protein, fat, vitamins and minerals.

Most people rely on a good brand of canned dog meat plus some plain biscuits.

◆ An active adult dog of Cocker Spaniel size, weighing about 14.5 kg (32 lb) will need each day one 376-g (13-oz) can of meat plus 175 g (6 oz) of biscuit meal and a few hard biscuits as treats.

◆ A 22.7 kg (50 lb) dog will need one-and-a-half to two cans of meat and the same volume of plain biscuit meal.

◆ Puppies cost relatively more to feed in their first year while they are growing. It should be possible to work out, from studying the prices of the dog foods on the supermarket shelves, the basic costs of feeding the dog you hope to have.

◆ **INSURANCE AND VET'S FEES**

Other necessary expenses will be insurance to cover the vet's costs for unexpected major illnesses and injuries; and veterinary fees for regular needs, such as vaccination, worming and anti-flea treatments.

◆ **EQUIPMENT**

You will also need to purchase some basic items of dog equipment, such as a folding crate, to be used as a movable bed; collars and leads; a basket or bed; food and water bowls; and a dog tag carrying your name and address.

◆ **KENNEL FEES**

If you go away on holiday and cannot take your dog with you, you may also have to pay boarding kennel fees for your dog.

DO SOME RESEARCH

As a prospective first-time dog owner, you should look around at your dog-owning friends, and at the local dogs in the park and at mixed breed shows held for charitable causes. Doubtless you will soon come to the conclusion that it would be lovely to have the constant companionship of a dog, and you will be absolutely right. But there is also a down side. Your dog will need companionship from you, and, at times, that may be inconvenient and will curb your own freedom. Puppies and adult dogs acquired from a rescue society will require a great deal of patience from you, the owner. Someone responsible must be there with the dog, and for the dog, for a good slice of all the daylight hours.

Puppies and dogs cannot train themselves; they need a sensible human on hand to teach them. If you take an adult dog from a rescue kennel, he may well need as much house and behaviour training as a puppy. You will probably have to begin all over again when a dog has spent some time in kennels and got used to a way of life where asking to go out is not part of the routine.

Kennelled dogs may bark constantly and cause complaints from your neighbours; and dogs put out in sheds and runs are not learning in-house behaviour, nor are they any deterrent to intruders.

DAYTIME SOLUTIONS
There are ways in which a working owner can manage to keep a dog, but having

Below: many dogs regard their crates as safe havens and dens, but they should not be used when the dog is left alone in the house.

someone 'pop in at lunchtime' is not a fail-safe solution. The 'popping in' time is all too short, and is mostly spent on clearing up what a puppy has done in a four-hour morning.

Some offices are sympathetic towards employees who take their dogs to work, especially if the dog is provided with a large folding plastic wire crate as a safe haven when the office gets too hectic.

The advantage of the wire crate is that the dog can see all that is happening, can be spoken to by passing humans, and the wire door can be left open or closed as suits the situation. Dogs love their crates; they act as a 'den' and a safe place in which to sleep and eat. The crates may seem expensive as an initial purchase, but in so many ways they are an invaluable aid to dog living, and much kinder, both at home and in the office, than shutting a dog away completely. However, a dog should never be shut into a crate when he is alone in the house; that is a cruelty.

LIVING ACCOMMODATION AND EXERCISE SPACE

Although it is theoretically possible to keep a dog in an apartment without a garden, such an arrangement would be excessively demanding on the owner, who must always be present to take the dog out for toileting, no matter what the weather or the owner's state of health. For a small dog, a tiny patio garden may

WORKING AT HOME

People who can work from home are ideally suited to have a dog, but it should be pointed out that the three to nine-months-old puppy stage can be very disruptive to a planned work schedule. However, your puppy will be house-trained all the quicker, and a little play in the garden is a great break for both dog and owner.

serve in an emergency, but it is cruel to confine a dog to a roof garden or a balcony for most of the time, and even more cruel to make a house-trained dog wait for the opportunity to urinate or defaecate. Although a routine can be established, sometimes dogs need to break their normal pattern, especially in illness. In summer, dogs like to alternate sitting in the sun with lying in the shade and they should have this freedom to follow their natural instincts.

THE GARDEN

Puppies almost certainly spoil a garden for a season or two. They dig, they race about, they bury their toys. If you have much-prized plants and vegetables you will have to fence them off, at least for the first year of dog ownership. Bitches ruin lawns with their urine puddle, but there are two alternative remedies.

Above: train your puppy to walk on a lead from the earliest possible age.

◆ Train your bitch, puppy or adult, to use a square of concrete or paving.
◆ Rush out with a bucket of water to put on the patch of grass the bitch has used.

Dogs will pick and eat soft fruit and apples, and they may dig up and gnaw at flower bulbs, especially daffodils, which are poisonous. It will not be possible to use many garden chemicals, especially slug pellets, which can be rapidly fatal to a dog.

Ponds and swimming pools are very dangerous for puppies, particularly if the water is covered in winter. Many puppies and young dogs are drowned every year by falling into straight-sided pools from which they cannot climb out. It takes a surprisingly short time for a young dog to drown. Make sure that all water is well fenced, at least for the first year of the pup's life.

EXERCISE AREAS

Where would you take your dog for a good run off the lead? Is there a safely-fenced park where dogs can run free nearby? Suitable places are becoming more difficult to find; some parks and beaches are forbidden to dogs, even when accompanied by their owners. Your dog must be completely under your control before you can contemplate letting him off the lead. Practise the 'come when called' routine (see page 74), giving lots of praise and a food reward when the dog comes instantly back to you. Mongrels are more difficult than pedigree dogs; their basic instinct is for unrestrained freedom and you must make being with you the most desirable choice.

Walking your dog off the lead in a town street or along a busy road is purely exhibitionism on the owner's part. There will always be some overwhelming distraction, which will cause the dog to disobey and run across the road. You also have to consider other walkers, who may feel reluctant to pass a dog that is not under full control. Extending leads are not the answer and can be dangerous.

FEAR AND DISLIKE OF DOGS

It has been calculated that at least half the British population do not like dogs, and that some of the 'dislikers' actually experience acute fear in the presence of even the most genial dogs. Are any of your regular visitors of this persuasion? It may not be a subject that has come up before, so it is worth finding out in advance so that you can plan a strategy if needed. Dogs quickly recognise people who are afraid of them, and their reaction may be to behave more aggressively than they would normally do. It can be a problem if visitors require the dog to be shut away; however, some dog-dislikers have been converted by meeting just one attractive puppy.

You may feel you are giving your dog a measure of freedom by having him on the full extent of a long lead, but he could ensnare other walkers by wrapping the lead around their legs.

You, as the owner, are liable for the damage your dog does to other people or their possessions. This is where your dog's insurance policy comes to your aid. Most policies, which are taken out primarily for veterinary fees, also carry substantial Third Party Cover. This is well worth having if you own a free-spirited kind of mongrel!

YOUR OWN LIFESTYLE

What are your interests and hobbies? Will you have to give up something you take pleasure in when you have your dog? For example, golf courses do not welcome dogs accompanying players. Although the idea of a dog running beside your horse when you go riding is an attractive one, there are few places where this can be done without prejudice to the safety of the dog, the horse, the riders and other road users. You are not fully in control of your dog when you are on top of a horse, and it is now an offence under the

Dangerous Dogs Act of 1991 not to have your dog under control at all times.

Jogging with your dog on the lead is not much fun for the dog. The canine joy is to pause and sniff around, not to keep up with the rhythm of your run.

Bring your picture of dog ownership up to date. There are comparatively few places now where a dog can run free safely. It must be said that many dogs do not enjoy walking on the lead for several miles, especially in very cold and wet conditions. Why not play with your dog in your own garden or even indoors? Retrieving games, hide and seek, or hunt the biscuit exercise the dog's mind as well as his body. This type of play helps to strengthen the bond between dog and owner and can be especially enjoyable for the older or inactive owner.

NEIGHBOURS

What is your relationship like with the people next door – good so far? If complaints are forthcoming about excessive barking, your dog invading their garden, breaking down their fence, jumping on their petunias or threatening their children or pets, a very worrying situation could blaze up surprisingly fast.

CHILDREN

If a dog is already established in the household, he can be taught to live in harmony with a baby and the pair can become very dear companions. But dogs and children should never be left together without some responsible supervision, and this is especially true if you plan to get a dog from a rescue home.

You will probably never know what painful and frightening experiences that dog has been through before you acquired him. You may find out a little by the way he reacts to certain objects or noises or even to some people, but you do not want to take the risk of triggering a past fear when the dog is alone with children.

Left: helping take care of a dog is a good learning experience for a child.

CHOOSING A DOG

Having decided that there is room, time and money for a dog in your life, your next consideration has to be not only 'I want a mongrel or a cross-breed', but also what kind of dog, what sex and what type of coat. These are crucial questions, apart from knowing whether you want a puppy or an adult.

TYPE OF COAT

If you want a long-coated pet, you have to enjoy grooming and you must have access to a place where you can do this twice-weekly chore. You will not want to groom a long-haired dog in your kitchen, so where can the job be done after dark on a winter's evening? Only you can

decide, but long coats do need attention if you are going to feel proud of your dog.

Puppies are not usually born with the type and length of coat that they will have when adult, so your only clue to what your dog will grow into has to be his mother. If the pup was randomly bred, then you probably have only half of the story, but that's what the luck of the mongrel is all about.

Right: thorough grooming is a soothing therapy for both the dog and his owner.

WHERE TO GET YOUR DOG?

There is a shortage of mongrel puppies and probably this trend will increase in the future. The reason is that people are obliged to take more care of their dogs and to prevent them from straying and siring litters. More than 400 Dog Wardens working in Britain say that dog owners are becoming more responsible. The other factor in reducing the number of mongrels is the neutering campaigns regularly set up and sponsored by rescue organisations like the RSPCA. Many charities insist that bitches are spayed before they can be re-homed, thereby limiting the number of mongrel pups available.

◆ Your best source of a healthy mongrel of good temperament is from a friend or a neighbour, whose bitch has had puppies which have been well reared and properly socialized from an early age. A family environment with children is the ideal birth place for a puppy, and it may be possible for you to be involved with the pup from very early in his life.

◆ Be prepared to wait for a puppy from such a good source; at least then you should get the pick of the litter and you may be able to suggest, if the breeder has not thought of it, that the pup is properly wormed and weaned on to good food before he comes to you.

◆ The next opportunity in your search is likely to be an advertisement for mongrel puppies in a local newspaper. Be selective. It has to be faced that some mongrels are kept in poor

Left: a healthy, well-groomed dog of good temperament is an object of pride for all the family.

conditions, and the bitch may not have been well fed in pregnancy or during the time she is feeding the puppies. A sickly puppy full of worms (toxocara canis) will need medical treatment. Harden your heart and walk away from the puppy if you have any doubts at all. If the dogs' conditions are awful, report them to your vet or the RSPCA. You may feel sorry for the puppies but buying a sick one could be time-consuming and expensive. Sickly puppies are not easy to put right and such a pup may be prone to disease all his life.

◆ Try the local veterinary surgeries. The staff there may know of a mongrel litter expected or already born. You will want to get your puppy examined by a vet anyway, as soon as you bring him home.

◆ The dog rescue charities sometimes have puppies available, either born on the premises from bitches handed over because they are pregnant, or they may have puppies of about eight weeks old, the remnants of litters which the breeder could not place. It is most rewarding if you can see the dam and get a report on her attitude and behaviour. Ask if the pups have been actively socialized, i.e. have they had the opportunity to hear lots of different household sounds and see and be seen by many different types of people, so that they are aware of the world outside the litter.

SOCIALIZATION

Puppies should be socialized from about three weeks of age, and this usually means they are kept in an enclosed area, in a house or a busy part of a rescue centre. Puppies that are reared in an isolated kennel will always be fearful and more dog orientated than people orientated.

You want your puppy or dog to become a junior member of your human family. Find out as much as you can about the parentage of the pup you are considering buying.

ADULT RESCUE DOGS

Choosing an adult dog from a rescue home is in some ways easier, as you can at least see the coat and the shape and size of the dogs on offer. But will you ever know what the dog's previous life has been, what he has learnt to be afraid of, what people or animals he is programmed to attack?

The staff of the rescue will have done some work with the dog and tried him out in a variety of situations, and with a number of different challenges. Even then, it may not be until you have had the dog in your own home for several weeks or even months that he reveals his true character. Always be vigilant, indoors and out, with your new adult pet, and never leave him alone with a baby or with older

Above: rather than buy a puppy, you can acquire an adult dog from a rescue society who is in need of a good home.

children until you are quite sure of his behaviour in any given circumstances. The dog cannot tell you, in so many words, the fears and torments he may have had to endure. You have to find out the hard way from his reactions. Many rescue societies will allow you to visit your prospective pet often and even to take the dog out on successive weekends until you are both really sure that you want to belong to each other.

ACQUIRING A PUPPY

So where will you get a puppy? Do try to buy him from the home in which he was born, because there you may judge the quality of care and also the amount of socialization the bitch and her pups have had. Ask at the local veterinary surgeries; they may well know where there is a litter. Also watch the columns of the local papers.

Dog rescue homes may also have puppies for sale, either from bitches which have been turned out because they were pregnant, or because the charity has been asked to take in the remaining members of a litter. You may also be able to partially reserve a pup from a litter not yet born.

The source of puppies to avoid is dealers, where the pups may have made long journeys from parts of the country where they are more difficult to sell. The pups may have been collected together to make up a van load, and this is always a major risk for transmitting disease. You will also not have the opportunity to see them with their dam – an even greater disadvantage than normal. When buying a mongrel you do need all the clues you can get as to what your dog may grow up to be.

USEFUL TIPS

◆ Whatever the source of your puppy, make sure he has been wormed once or twice before you collect him, which will usually be when he is about seven to eight weeks old.

◆ The puppy should be able to eat solid food, and should walk, run and be ready to respond to your offer to play.

◆ If you have the choice of the litter, it may well be wise not to take the boldest one; 'the one that comes towards you' used to be the received wisdom. Do not take a pup that hangs back and appears shy and reluctant to leave his bed.

◆ Choose the middle-of-the-range puppy, which should mean a dog which is not too outgoing, nor too retiring. Never, ever, ever, take a puppy which is obviously sick or is deformed in some

SPAYING A BITCH

If you take a bitch puppy from a rescue home you will probably have to promise to get her neutered (spayed) at a future date. Spaying a mongrel bitch will save you all the worry of the times when she would come into season, and the unwanted attention of male dogs. Spayed bitches are also saved from life-threatening diseases of the uterus, and have a reduced risk of developing mammary cancers.

way, just because your heart goes out to him and you feel that he needs you. The right answer for a weak puppy is for him to remain with the breeder. Never begin your dog ownership with an unhealthy puppy; it is not fair to yourself, your friends or the puppy. It is a mistake to think that imperfect puppies are going to be small, sweet and compliant. Very often pain can trigger aggression and bad temper, and in addition there may be difficulty with other dogs, who can be motivated to turn upon a weak member of the pack. You could be buying a lot of heartbreak and expense in trying to treat a puppy that never was sound.

PAYING FOR YOUR PUPPY

We have spoken of buying a puppy, and that is the right expression. Properly reared puppies have cost the breeder something, and there is a strong feeling that dogs which are given away are not so valued as dogs who have been paid for; whether from a private home or a welfare kennel, expect to pay for your new pet.

Left: be prepared to wait for the right puppy for your family and make sure that he is healthy and strong.

ACQUIRING AN ADULT DOG

Would you rather have an adult dog? There is plenty of choice, with young, middle-aged and even older mongrels in the rescue homes. You may find that the rescue charities insist that both dogs and bitches are neutered before they leave their care. Normally dogs from rescue charities are only 'lent' to new owners and it is usual to find that the charity retains the nominal ownership of the dog and the right to repossess him if the dog is unhappy or badly treated, but otherwise he is completely your pet. You will probably have the advantage of being able to go back to the rescue home to get advice if you find that your dog suffers from phobias or unreasonable fears which trigger difficult behaviour patterns.

You will be able to find out as much of the dog's history as the charity knows, and you may be able to make some trial visits and even take the dog out for walks before you make your choice. You will undoubtedly be asked a number of questions about your home, your life and your family before being granted a dog, and it may be that you feel that these questions are somewhat intrusive. Please be tolerant; the animal charities have a responsibility to place the dogs that have come into their care in good, permanent homes with new understanding owners.

Will you adopt a dog or a bitch? Both are likely to be neutered but the dog will probably always retain a strain of assertiveness, and the bitch is likely to be more biddable.

It would be wrong to give the impression that taking an adult dog will be the easy option. This is unlikely to be true of a dog that has been running free, or has been abandoned by previous owners, or indeed given to the rescue home because he is unmanageable in

Left: taking your dog home is the beginning of a long, happy partnership.

some way. Probably the kennel staff will have done some work with such a dog and will be able to tell you something about the way the dog behaves with other animals, and with men, women and children. Spend some time with the dog you are considering. Ask to be allowed to take him into the grounds of the rescue home on your own, always keeping the dog on the lead and noting his reactions to all your approaches.

ASSESSING A RESCUE DOG'S TEMPERAMENT

1 Try to have the dog you are attracted to in a separate room with no more than two adults present (not kennel staff). Children should not be included.

2 Sit quietly for ten minutes, not speaking to the dog, but watching his reaction to you. Do not make eye contact. See if he is curious enough to approach you.

3 Extend the back of your hand to the dog for him to sniff.

4 If the dog appears interested and friendly, look at him while you offer your hand again.

5 Offer a small piece of biscuit. Does the dog fear you, does he snatch the food, does he refuse? These reactions do not preclude taking the dog; they indicate the areas you will have to work on.

6 If the dog is friendly towards you, squat down and see if he will come to you. Offer a tug toy and see if the dog is confident enough to play.

7 At another testing session, come in very nonchalantly while brandishing a walking stick or an umbrella. Does the dog panic?

8 Make a reverberant noise by banging lightly on a metal object or something similar.

9 Ask if you may observe the dog's behaviour when he is outside in a run with some other dogs.

10 Ask the staff if they have had the dog in the reception area or in the recreation room with them.

11 Try putting a lead on the dog and try to talk him into going out with you.

12 Take the dog for a short walkabout, put him back into the kennel and then invite him to come out again.

◆ All the while, without appearing to focus on the dog, you will be observing his behaviour patterns – not expecting any kind of perfection but looking for any negative reactions that may have to be overcome. Only after you have won the dog's confidence will you feel you can introduce children of various ages. Expect to make these exploratory meetings over a period of days or weeks. When you find that the dog is looking out for you and really pleased to see you, you will realise you have the basis of a good dog/human relationship.

◆ Dogs recognise tone of voice and facial expressions, so keep your voice light and happy even if the dog shows hostility. Dogs can smell fear and aggression so your approach must always be warm, light and inconsequential. If the dog is constantly unfriendly, make no response and walk away; never show anger that your offer of friendship has been rejected.

◆ Try again on another day and continue until the dog is used to seeing you and has convinced himself that you mean him no threat and no harm.

Above and right: spend lots of time playing with your new puppy and getting to know each other. Make a fuss of him and reward him with cuddles when he obeys your commands.

BUYING A PUPPY

Puppies are born in a very unfinished state, without sight or hearing, and needing the stimulation of their dam's tongue in order to urinate or defaecate. Puppies are able to cry, and to crawl on their abdomens, but are not capable of keeping themselves warm unless they are adjacent to a source of heat. At birth their lungs are immature and their hearts have a lot of adjustment to make. Within three to four weeks, however, those same puppies will have developed into active, all-seeing, all-hearing, all-barking little monsters, being weaned onto solid food, anxious to explore their environment and everything within it. Another week will have them playing actively with the rest of the litter, and with toys, growling, barking and responding to the sound of their breeder's voice. At this stage they can recognise their own need to pass urine and faeces and will be motivated to move away from their sleeping area to do so. In fact, the puppies have reached the stage, well within two months, that we might expect a human baby to reach at two years old.

HEALTH PROBLEMS

Some of the puppies may be born with imperfections, possibly due to an infection which the bitch may have picked up while they were developing in the uterus. Often defects are not noticed until the puppies begin to be active. Examine them carefully for any imperfections before you make your choice.

◆ **HERNIAS**
Probably the most common congenital defects are hernias, either at the navel (an umbilical hernia) or in the groin (an inguinal hernia). A hernia is a protrusion of a part of the body's organs through a weakness in the surrounding tissue. There may be a need for a surgical repair later on if the hernia grows larger.

◆ **CLEFT PALATE**
A cleft palate is the result of a failure of the hard palate, on the roof of the mouth, to fuse properly. The breeder will no doubt have noticed early on that the puppy was unable to suck properly from the bitch, and may have been very difficult to rear and appear under-nourished in comparison with the rest of the litter. The breeder is the best person to cope with a puppy with a major defect such as this; do not be persuaded into taking such a puppy, even as a gift.

◆ **CHEST PROBLEMS**
When you pick a puppy up, you may hear a wheezing or rattling sound in his

chest. This may be because his lungs may not have expanded properly at birth, or because fluid has got down into the chest. Ask for a veterinary examination before deciding to take on such a puppy.

◆ LAMENESS

Often puppies are a little unsteady on their feet at first, but let the puppy you are considering run about on the floor alone and watch carefully for persistent lameness on one leg, or a tendency to fall over frequently. Leave this puppy with the breeder.

◆ JUVENILE PYODERMA

This is a rash of tiny pus-filled spots often on the hairless parts of the abdomen or in the groin. This is thought to be caused by a failure of the bitch to clean the puppies sufficiently well, or possibly comes from the use of old newspaper as bedding for the puppies. The rash should clear up with more attention to hygiene and bathing with antiseptic lotion, but antibiotics may be needed also. Ask for veterinary advice before buying the puppy. You will usually find the whole litter has the rash. This may be a reason for taking your puppy away as early as seven weeks of age in order to improve his living conditions.

◆ BODY TREMORS

Many puppies shake and twitch while they are asleep; this is natural and is thought to be connected with the developing nervous system. However, a state of low blood sugar, brought on by stress and excitement, may cause whole body tremors which may lead to convulsions. This condition may occur during play when the puppy first changes home and is made an object of everyone's attention. Give the puppy a drink of honey and water, and report to a veterinary surgeon at once.

◆ THE URINARY SYSTEM

Sometimes the urinary system may be imperfectly developed in puppies, but this condition might go unnoticed while the pups are together in the litter. A constant uncontrolled dribbling of urine may result

from a defect in the urinary system so that urine produced in the kidneys by-passes the bladder and consequently it cannot be stored. This condition, which tends to occur in female puppies, can be corrected by surgery. Urine scalding on the abdomen of a puppy is painful and unpleasant. The cause should be investigated by a veterinary surgeon.

◆ DIGESTIVE SYSTEM

When you go to see puppies aged around six weeks old, see if you can arrange to be there when they are fed. Pups of this age are usually fed from a communal dish, so watch which ones are greedy and which seem reluctant to eat. Puppies always defaecate immediately after their meal, and this is an important clue to the health of the litter. The bowel motions should be formed, not loose, unless the pups have been wormed that day. Diarrhoea is a common but undesirable condition in puppies. There may be many causes for this: possibly a change of diet, unwise feeding, a heavy worm infestation, the result of a worming dose, or a disease, such as the easily transmissible canine parvovirus. If the whole litter is seen to pass loose, blood-stained motions, go no further with your interest in buying one of these puppies and please disinfect your shoes and clothes before visiting any other breeders.

Canine parvovirus is a dreadful disease and is very difficult to eradicate once it is endemic in a dog sanctuary or a dealer's kennels.

Do not take away a puppy which is producing loose motions, but, as this may only be a temporary state, arrange to visit again in three or four days.

INFECTIOUS DISEASES

Eyes and nose running with mucus? Distemper is still a very real disease, especially among mongrels. Kennel cough may also be present where there is a constantly changing population of dogs. This airborne virus is easily transmissible and it can last a very long time and even be fatal in puppies.

The typical cough sounds as if the dog has got something stuck in his throat. If you hear such a cough, take no notice of any excuses that may be made – leave in a hurry.

FEEDING YOUR DOG

Do not be tempted to feed your dog or puppy on demand. A greedy dog will keep on eating, and you must control your dog's weight. Here are some general guidelines to help you.

FEEDING A PUPPY

◆ As a general rule, most eight-week-old puppies are fed four times a day, reducing to three times (but increasing the quantity given) at twelve weeks old.

◆ An average quantity of food at each meal would be 150 g (5 oz), two-thirds of which should be bread or plain biscuit meal and one-third, meat, cooked egg or cheese.

◆ Keep the feeding times regular and always provide clean, fresh water. Puppies do not need milk after eight weeks, and large quantities can act as a laxative.

◆ Do not offer food straight from the refrigerator; always warm it to blood heat.

◆ Make sure that no other animal can take the pup's food and ensure that he does not feel threatened while he is eating.

◆ If, after 10 minutes, the puppy has not eaten all the food in his dish, remove it and throw it away. Do not give him anything else to eat until the next feeding time becomes due.

◆ Sometimes puppies have sore mouths when they are cutting their second teeth – at four to eight months old. Puréeing the food may make it more palatable.

FEEDING AN ADULT DOG

◆ The easiest way to feed your adult dog is to use commercially prepared canned or dried foods from a leading manufacturer. There are feeding instructions on the packaging and most companies also employ specialist nutritionists whom you can consult if you have problems.

◆ Many owners feel that they must offer a dog as much variety of food as they have themselves, but this is a fallacy. If a dog likes a particular dried or canned food, he will eat it every day for most of his life.

◆ Most owners add a few household scraps to enliven a dried diet, but the dog does not really need them. Cheese, a cooked egg and vegetables of all kinds are useful as titbits but beware of giving highly spiced foods.

◆ A medium-sized adult dog will eat one to one-and-a-half standard-sized 376-g (12-oz) cans of meat and an equal volume of biscuit every day, divided into two meals. A benefit of using quality commercially prepared diets is that they contain a perfect balance of essential vitamins and minerals. You have no need to add more.

◆ Dogs are usually fed twice a day: morning and evening. The timing should be kept as regular as possible.

◆ If you are feeding a dried food, you will notice that your dog drinks more than when on a softer diet. The dry food acts as a cleaner for the teeth and gums, but some dogs do prefer their meals to be moist, so soak the dry food in some water, stock or thin gravy before feeding.

◆ Food refusal in a healthy dog is always a matter for concern, but one day does not really matter. Keep a close eye on the dog. Pain, shown by rolling and moaning, or by going into the prayer position (down on his front legs but with the abdomen elevated and the hind legs in standing attitude) should not be allowed to continue for more than two to three hours. Telephone your vet immediately.

◆ Some dogs are fussy eaters. For instance, some will not eat when there are unfamiliar people in the house, or when there is excessive noise. In some dogs, guarding comes first, and food can wait until the assumed danger is over. Some male dogs will stop eating temporarily when a bitch close-by is in season.

◆ You may notice that your dog is only willing to take food into one side of his mouth. Take him to the vet at once so that the condition can be properly investigated.

◆ Sick dogs appreciate having their food liquidized for softer eating. Favourite foods in illness are white fish or chicken with cooked rice or mashed potato. Meat soup and egg custard are also appreciated. Hand-feeding is often necessary when dogs are ill.

They will take food from the owner's hand when they will not eat it off a plate.

FEEDING AN ELDERLY DOG

◆ Old dogs need special cosseting and often special meals. You may find your dog prefers four small meals a day rather than two large ones, and that liquidized or very finely chopped food is more acceptable.

◆ Teeth can be painful or there may be growths in the mouth, so do not expect your geriatric friend to eat hard biscuit.

◆ Older dogs need less protein than growing animals in order to relieve stress on their ageing kidneys. The brand of food you have been using may be available in a special formula for elderly dogs.

◆ Some older dogs suffer from arthritis of the spine and they find bending to the floor to eat very uncomfortable. It is possible to buy metal bowl stands which raise the food bowl 17.5-20 cm (7-8 in) above floor level.

BUYING AN ADULT DOG

The health of adults is easier to check. Look for clear eyes, reasonably sweet breath, clean teeth, and a good clean coat. Bright pink mucus membranes and insides of ears and lips are not good signs, especially in a white dog, which may be suffering from an allergy that is expensive to diagnose and treat.

One feature that is important to check in male puppies over three months old and in adult dogs is whether there are two testicles which are descended into the scrotum. The testicles normally come down when the puppy is between six and twelve weeks old, and sometimes even older, but occasionally, one testicle is permanently retained in the abdominal cavity, and there is the possibility that this testicle can become cancerous. Many veterinary surgeons will suggest that a retained testicle is removed surgically before it gives any trouble.

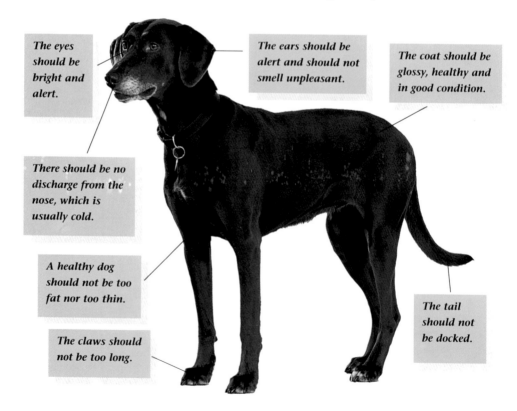

The eyes should be bright and alert.

The ears should be alert and should not smell unpleasant.

The coat should be glossy, healthy and in good condition.

There should be no discharge from the nose, which is usually cold.

A healthy dog should not be too fat nor too thin.

The tail should not be docked.

The claws should not be too long.

PUPPY MAINTENANCE

Get ready for your new puppy or your dog, well ahead of the proposed collection date. You can start by checking out your home and garden thoroughly to ensure that everything is safe and secure.

YOUR GARDEN

◆ Check your fencing, remembering that puppies can squeeze through very small holes and will also dig under wire or wooden fencing. Ideally the fence should be inserted 15 cm (6 in) into the ground.

◆ Check access to any water features in the garden, such as ponds and swimming pools. Ideally, they should be fenced in or surrounded by walls.

◆ Make sure any poisonous substances, such as slug bait, Warfarin rat poison or alphachloralose mouse poison, are on very high shelves in your shed or garage. Check also that none of the poisons have been laid around your garden. Paraquat weed killer is especially dangerous. The packaging of some slug baits and pesticides may state that the preparation is safe to use where there are household pets, but you cannot be too careful, and puppies will eat anything to excess. Many of the slug preparations have a sweet taste which dogs seem unable to resist. Anti-freeze liquid, and anything containing lead, such as old paint, can be poisonous.

◆ The seeds, flowers and the bark of the laburnum tree have been known to cause fatalities in pets. Flower bulbs, such as

daffodils and hyacinths, are dangerous and are just the kind of thing that a puppy will chew. At Christmastime beware of the berries of holly and mistletoe, and the leaves of the poinsettia plant.

◆ Take a look at access to any roads from your garden. Fence the front garden as well as the back, and check the gate catches. They should shut easily and quickly behind callers so that the pup has no opportunity to slip out. Take particular care of the security of any gate between the front and the back of your house, especially if it is used by other people.

◆ This is the time to tidy away dumps of disused materials, such as old tins of paint, discarded wood with nails sticking out, old car batteries, and plastic containers which once contained corrosive material. You may be sure the puppy will get at anything you do not want him to. Be sure there are no shards of broken glass or china near the surface of the earth.

Parts of some very old gardens were once used as rubbish dumps for broken utensils, and after rain these pieces tend to come to the surface. Even a tiny piece of glass can cut a dog's foot.

Old baths used in the garden and water butts need protecting too.

◆ Keep the puppy indoors when you are using any sprays on plants or spreading any top dressings. Puppies and adult dogs do tend to eat horse manure spread on the garden, but it seems to do them no harm.

INDOOR HAZARDS

Indoors, beware of electrical connections. Make sure that there are no dangling flexes or plug points at floor level which the puppy can reach.

◆ Kitchen cupboards must be fitted with secure fastenings or you may come home to find the puppy has

Left: woven baskets are difficult to clean and get destroyed very easily. A plastic bed is a better choice for durability.

Left: 'dog friendly' safe toys are durable and can give many hours of pleasure and comfort to a dog in the owner's absence.

book which get chewed. The habit of not leaving possessions around has to be learnt by adults and children alike, because it is unfair to be angry with the puppy for tearing up something which could just as easily have been put out of his reach.

created a mixture of raw potatoes, sugar, flour and haricot beans – not a good idea!

◆ The cupboard under the sink, where cleaning fluids and soaps are kept, is probably the most dangerous of all. Dogs are attracted by soap, so make sure none is accessible in the bathroom, cloakroom or kitchen. A tablet of soap taken into the mouth and foaming up when mixed with saliva can easily choke a dog to death.

◆ Make sure the puppy cannot get at the washing machine outlet. Many hoses are chewed through by pups.

◆ When leaving a puppy alone in the kitchen or utility room it is best to turn off the source of electricity from all apparatus, and never leave electrical equipment plugged into the sockets.

◆ Puppies and dogs are most likely to chew the articles which their owner has handled recently. This is why it is always the new shoes, or the most recently read

TOYS

◆ A puppy needs lots of suitable toys, just as a child does. Buy toys that are sturdy and tough, designed and created for dogs. Be especially wary of toys that include squeakers; these may over-excite

CHOKING

If you play with your dog with a ball, make sure it is of a size which is too big to obstruct the back of his throat – choking on a ball is not uncommon and requires immediate first aid. Get behind the dog and with one hand on each side of the head, push forward sharply so that the ball is ejected. Trying to reach inside the mouth does little to help, as there is too much saliva, but you may be able to get hold of the ball with cooking tongs.

a puppy or dog which has terrier ancestry, as the squeak can invoke a killing instinct. Squeakers are easily removed from toys and may be swallowed, causing serious damage to the dog.

◆ A piece of cotton cloth which is large enough not to be swallowed gives great pleasure to a puppy, as does a length of tough rope for tugging games.

GATES, PENS AND CRATES

◆ A baby gate can be invaluable in confining a puppy in a room without shutting him away from human company. It can also be used at the bottom of the stairs to stop the puppy rampaging all over the bedrooms. If he does scramble upstairs, help him to come down safely until he is big enough to cope on his own.

Baby gates and folding wire crates help to confine the pup to certain areas of the house safely. Puppies need to be able to see other people and hear lots of sounds while being absolutely secure from harm. A wire crate is a splendid investment, used as a

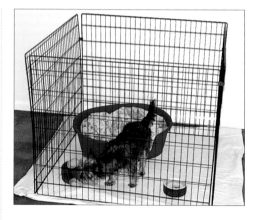

Above: a pen can be a comfortable and safe den for a young puppy.

bed and as a den, with the door open so that the puppy can go in and out as he wishes, or with the door closed as a temporary safety zone when there is activity in the house which might lead to a dangerous situation for him. Never confine the puppy to the crate for long periods; that can be cruel, and it ruins house-training and teaches the puppy nothing.

BEDS AND BEDDING

If you do not have a crate, a cardboard box of suitable size, with an entrance cut away at the front, will make an excellent bed for a puppy. You may wish to put the bed into an enclosure in the kitchen. Two or three pieces of the polyester fur called 'Vet

Bed' will make the best dog and puppy bedding. This fur is white and washes and dries like magic. It lasts for many years, is practically non-destructible and is a really worthwhile investment. If you decide to use discarded clothing in your puppy's bed, make sure that buttons and zips are removed before the puppy undertakes this job himself.

COLLAR AND LEAD

◆ You also need a leather collar of an appropriate size for an adult dog (the rescue home will probably sell you one), or a softer collar for a puppy. With these collars go leather leads with secure hooks.

◆ An extending lead, contained in a box handle, which you can let out or pull in at will can be useful if you want to give a confirmed roamer a little more range, but these leads should never be used in towns as they can easily prove an obstruction and cause an accident if the lead becomes wound round a passer-by.

IDENTITY TAGS

Possibly your most important buy of all is a name tag engraved with your name and telephone number. Get this done even before you get your puppy, as it is the law

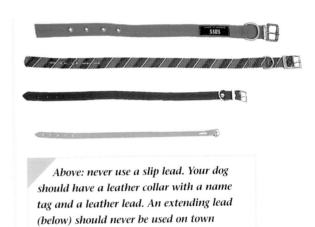

Above: never use a slip lead. Your dog should have a leather collar with a name tag and a leather lead. An extending lead (below) should never be used on town pavements where it might trip passers-by.

that it must always be worn when your dog is outside your own home, or is in your car. A name tag with your current address can save your dog's life, so check on it often, to ensure that the engraving is still legible. Most pet shops will be able to direct you to a source of name tags, and some charities and pet insurance companies supply them to subscribers.

MICROCHIPPING

Thousands of pets are lost every year – a tragedy which can happen to the most careful owner. Many of these animals are never re-united

with their owners. The RSPCA believes that the best way to avoid losing your pet is to have him implanted with a specially-developed microchip 'tag'. This provides a permanent link between you and your pet.

The chip's code is held on a national computer network which keeps a record of an owner's name and address. The RSPCA, as well as veterinary surgeons and local authority dog wardens, has scanners which can read the microchip's code.

Microchipping is no more complicated than a normal injection. A tiny microchip – the size of a grain of rice – is inserted under your pet's skin. The one-off cost can vary but it is not expensive. Contact your veterinary surgeon if you decide to have your dog microchipped.

GROOMING EQUIPMENT

A pet shop will also help you to choose the right type of brush and comb for your dog's coat. Even if your puppy does not have much coat to groom, start doing it regularly from the time he comes to you so that grooming time will become an evjoyable habit for you both.

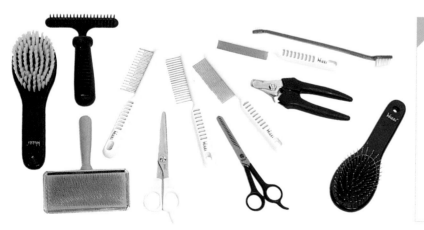

Left: you will need some grooming tools to remove dead hair from your dog's coat. Ask your vet which ones are most suitable for your dog. Use a toothbrush to clean his teeth and ask the practice nurses how to cut his nails.

CREATING CONFIDENCE

One of your primary tasks is to give your puppy or your adult dog confidence in you and other people. Puppies are at their most impressionable between eight and twelve weeks old, and the experiences encountered at this time must all be happy ones.

◆ You will obviously need to prevent a puppy doing damage to your furnishings but do it in a happy way; distract the pup with a food treat and direct his attention to some occupation that is permissible. You may well have to do the same thing for an adult dog which has spent some time in a rescue home.

◆ Always speak to your dog in a happy voice – never shout – and make a great fuss of your dog or puppy when he comes to you when you call him.

◆ You, first of all, and then members of your family and callers to your home must all be good news for your dog.

◆ Never allow anyone to tease the dog or pretend to threaten him. Such behaviour could have dangerous consequences, particularly if you have a rescue dog who has had a bad time in his past.

THE LANGUAGE

You must have just one more family conference before you collect the puppy which is to be yours. Perhaps you need not decide on the puppy's name until he is in your home so that you can choose something really appropriate, but do decide on the other words you are going to use to train the puppy so that everyone in the household, or those who are going to meet the puppy, will be talking the same language. Puppies respond to sounds so you must all use the same ones.

Which words will you use for 'Come here', 'Go away', 'Lie down', 'Sit', and for the all-important toilet-training sequence? It is sensible not to use nursery terminology here as passers-by may

be amused. The Guide Dogs for the Blind Association teach new owners to say 'Hurry up'.

My dogs respond to 'Go and be good', but there are lots of variants you may try. I knew of one dog that would urinate in response to a special whistle. Your task in re-training an adult mongrel may be difficult, given the free-running spirit of many of these dogs, and the time they have spent in kennels. Consistency is the secret; take the dog to the same spot every time and wait around, offering him encouragement, until he performs and then be lavish with your praise.

If your dog should defaecate in the street or in a public open space, never

Above: when toilet-training your puppy, always take him outside.

reproach him – he has probably been doing this all his life. Try to prevent it happening again by giving him the opportunity to use your own garden before you go for a walk. However, if the worst happens, be ready with a small plastic bag over your hand to scoop up the mess and pop the bag and contents into a plastic carrier. Tie the handles together, ready to put into the first appropriate refuse bin. When you are house-training your puppy at home, you should follow the same regime.

COLLECTING YOUR PUPPY

It is best to arrange to collect your puppy or your adult dog in the morning, and then you will have the whole day to get acquainted. Most people opt for collection on a Saturday so that they have the whole weekend. Some take a week's holiday to get to know their puppy.

◆ You should have inquired well ahead of this time what food the puppy has been weaned on, so that you can get a supply of the cereal and the meat, or the dry food mix to which the puppy is accustomed. Ask to see the consistency of the food that has been given and the amount for each meal. It is wise to keep the puppy on this food for a few days when he first comes to your home, even if you mean to make changes later.

◆ The biggest change for the puppy will be in getting used to being a single individual instead of one of a litter. Whatever the pleasures you can offer, the loss of the companionship and support of litter-mates is deeply felt. However, so is the compounded excitement of being in a new environment and with new people. So keep the food and the feeding times to what the puppy has been used to. The

VACCINATION

All puppies must be vaccinated against the following dangerous infectious diseases:
- Distemper
- Canine parvovirus
- Hepatitis
- Leptospirosis
- Kennel cough

These vaccines are usually given in a two- or three-stage course. You may find that your eight-week-old puppy has had only the first injection and your own vet will have to complete the course. Adult dogs should also have annual boosters for the same diseases as immunity does wane in time. It may be that you will be told that your puppy has been vaccinated and you will be required to pay for this protection. Make sure that you receive a proper printed vaccination certificate which has been signed by a veterinary surgeon, then, in the rare cases where something does go wrong, you have some proof to produce.

Do not rely on homeopathic vaccination routines; this is one area of homeopathy which is not always effective and this type of vaccination is not accepted by boarding kennels. They will not take in dogs which have not had conventional vaccination.

same advice, in a modified way, will also apply to an adult dog. When taking a puppy it is useful if the breeder can show you how much food the puppy has been accustomed to eating at each meal.

THE JOURNEY HOME

It is usual to collect a puppy or adult dog by car and this is much easier if there are two people involved: one to hold the puppy on their lap and the other to drive.

Take with you on the collection journey a towel to cover your lap, a lot of kitchen roll to clean up accidents, and a small dish and a bottle of water if the journey is at all long. Expect to pay the asking price for the puppy or dog on collection, and make sure you get a receipt. Do not let an adult

mongrel out for a run on the way home – you do not belong to him yet and he is very likely to run off.

ARRIVING HOME

Resist the temptation to take your puppy to show friends and relatives, or to ask them to come round when you get home. Take things slowly; do not overwhelm the puppy, or the adult dog for that matter, with new experiences all on the same day.

Give your new pet time to adjust to you, your family, and your house, and keep excitement to a minimum. Let the dog explore on his own, while you watch discreetly. Call him back to you often. If you have a small puppy, go down on your haunches and welcome him with open arms – your delight in each other will be mutual.

FIRST NIGHTS

Probably the first crisis in a young puppy's life will come at the end of the first day with you. He may have fallen into several deep sleeps during the day, but by nightfall he will be worn out by his many new experiences. You may settle the

Left: when you arrive home, spend some time getting to know your new puppy.

HEALTH CHECKS

You would be wise to take your new puppy to a veterinary surgeon for a health check. Many people arrange to go into the vet's on their way back from collecting the puppy. The advantage is that you can be assured that he is sound and healthy, and if a major fault is found, you can go back to the breeder straight away without the risk of taking infectious disease into your home.

Ask the vet about anti-flea and louse treatments for both the puppy and your home, and, if you live in chalk country, mention the dreaded Trombicula (harvest mites) too. Most sunny summers bring a plague of these bright pink parasites which cause intense itching to both humans and dogs, but they can be killed by special anti-parasitic treatments.

This is the time to ask about pet insurance for veterinary fees. Vaccination and flea treatments are not covered by any company's policies, but bills for surgery and medical treatment for illness can soon mount up. Ask which insurance company is the most effective in terms of accepting claims and paying them promptly as well as for charging reasonable premiums and deducting the least excess charge.

puppy in his bed with a well-covered hot water bottle for him to cuddle up to. The practice of putting a ticking clock nearby to keep him company has gone out of style, as too many puppies took the clock to pieces during the night!

Cover the floor around the puppy's bed thickly with newspaper and creep off to your own bed hoping that the pup will sleep until morning. Unfortunately, this is rarely the case. Puppies in the nest are accustomed to waking in the night and having a little play session together before going back to sleep. If your puppy wakes he will find that he is cold, in a strange environment which does not smell familiar, and he will feel desperately lonely and disorientated. Much the same may be true of the adult dog which has been in kennels for some time.

Your new member of the family needs company. The solution is for him to sleep close to you, preferably in a high-sided box beside your bed. When your new friend stirs and begins to cry, you are there to offer comfort and reassurance. If you think it necessary, you can take him into the garden to relieve himself. Take a torch or turn on the outside lighting so that you can locate your dog in the dark.

HEALTH AND CONDITION

The eyes are a very good indicator of a dog's condition. Runny eyes or a nose exuding mucous demand instant advice. Telephone the vet and arrange an appointment.

◆ Run your hands over your dog frequently, identifying any lumps and bumps. Is it a tick embedded in the flesh? Is it a thistle head? Is it a wart or another skin condition? Do not let any blemish like this go unnoticed for long. Persistent scratching, biting the feet, or shaking the ears can be annoying to the owner and exasperating to the dog.

◆ An invasion of parasites may be the cause; or there may be an ear or tooth disease. Get a diagnosis quickly before the condition becomes chronic.

PARASITES

Most local councils are tolerant of any well-contained dog faeces being put into domestic waste bins. Never incorporate them in a compost heap or dig them into the garden. If there are any roundworm eggs in the faeces they will develop in time and will infect your ground. The roundworm larvae (Toxocara canis) can infect children – for example, if they eat without washing their hands after playing in the garden. Generally, the larvae pass harmlessly out of the human body but occasionally they will embed themselves in an organ of the body and this can lead to serious disease. The larvae cannot cause the threadworms (pin worms) which so often infect young children when they start school. This is a completely separate parasite, passed from human to human and never via dogs or cats.

Nevertheless, it is important to worm dogs and puppies regularly and to dispose of the excreta afterwards effectively. It is always best to get the worming preparation from a veterinary surgery so that you get a dosage which is effective but not so strong as to upset the animal. It may be useful to know that freshly passed dog faeces are not a medium by which Toxocara canis may be transmitted. The larvae need time to mature, possibly weeks or months, depending upon weather conditions, and all signs of the actual faeces will have disappeared by the time the larvae are capable of doing harm.

FEEDING

It is usual to feed eight-week-old puppies four times daily, with clean water always available for drinking. Puppies do not need milk; in fact, it can bring on diarrhoea. The choice of foods lies mainly with canned foods which are labelled 'complete', which means you do not need to give anything else; or dried complete foods, which are usually moistened with warm water for puppies.

◆ You will find that many brands of dog food provide a range of 'age-designed' foods, i.e. for growing puppies, adult dogs, elderly dogs and dogs not taking much exercise.

◆ It is easier for the owner and better for the puppy to feed a commercially formulated

WORMING

A puppy should have been wormed at least once, preferably twice, before he leaves his first home. Ask the breeder when he was wormed and which preparation was used, so that you can tell your vet when you take the puppy for his first health check and vaccination.

It is possible that even if a worming preparation was given, the puppy may have brought it up again. It will usually be necessary to worm the puppy again, but wait until the vet can weigh him and prescribe the appropriate dose. If you take an adult dog from a rescue centre, remember to check up on the worming routine.

food which is balanced with all the necessary vitamins and minerals, and which carries instructions about the quantity to feed on the label. If you are in any doubt, the nurses or receptionists at your veterinary surgery will be only too glad to help you.

◆ Keep a close eye on your new puppy or adult dog during the first few days and weeks he is with you. Diarrhoea is probably the most alarming sign that all is not well with a pup. It may be that you are giving too much food, or too many unsuitable titbits; or indeed someone else may, out of kindness, be offering the dog enticing but inappropriate food.

◆ Watch the puppy closely to see if he is demonstrating any signs of acute abdominal pain? One of the signs is going into the 'prayer position' – down on the front legs, which will be stretched out before him, but with the abdomen and back legs held high.

◆ Try a teaspoonful of gripe water, as given to human babies, and if this does not give relief, make an appointment and take the puppy to the vet straight away. It

Above: dog diets labelled 'complete' come in various textures, and with a balanced content for growing puppies and adults. A good brand will contain all the protein, fat, carbohydrate, vitamins and minerals that your dog needs at every stage of his life.

may be that he has snatched something, such as a plastic toy or nylon tights, which is causing an obstruction in the gut and will require veterinary help to clear.

◆ Diarrhoea, without obvious pain, will often clear up if you miss out one meal and then give the dog a very bland diet, such as cooked chicken with plain boiled rice, for a couple of days. Always provide drinking water. It is harmful to limit water in the hope that it may 'dry up' diarrhoea.

◆ If the diarrhoea is persistent or if the puppy becomes ill, you should take him to the vet. If vomiting accompanies the diarrhoea, seek veterinary advice.

THE VETERINARY WORLD

It may be useful here to look at the organisation of the veterinary profession in Britain. No-one except a qualified veterinary surgeon is permitted by law to diagnose and treat animals, so beware of asking or taking unauthorised advice from any other source. Veterinary surgeons carry the initials of the college from which they graduated after their name, and also the letters M.R.C.V.S. (Member of the Royal College of Veterinary Surgeons), or F.R.C.V.S. (Fellow of the Royal College of Veterinary Surgeons) for those of higher qualification.

Veterinary surgeons, and nowadays more than fifty per cent are women, work in practices. They may be single handed, or four or five or even more vets working together, but all are small businesses, setting their own charges and arranging their own working hours as suits their locality best. There are no standard charges of cost, but pet owners can always ask for an estimate for any course of care.

Veterinary surgeons very rarely make house calls these days, as they can deal with illness or accidents much better in the surgery where they have all their specialist equipment to hand and probably qualified nurses to assist them. So if you need to consult a vet, you should telephone and make an appointment to take your dog to the surgery.

Veterinary surgeons dispense all the medications they prescribe from the surgery, and your bill will include all medication and dressings. Note that VAT will be added. The Royal College of Veterinary Surgeons obliges all practices to provide a twenty-four hour service of care to animals, but where practices are small you may find that several combine to provide night cover in their area. If you need a vet outside normal consulting hours, or at the weekend, you may find you are transferred to an unfamiliar practice, but not too far away.

If your dog has a medical condition which becomes complicated, then your veterinary surgeon may suggest referral to a specialist vet in a particular discipline, such as orthopaedics, ophthalmology or dermatology. Specialists have undertaken their postgraduate study to either R.C.V.S. certificate or diploma level in their particular specialization. You are entitled to suggest to your general practitioner vet that you would like your pet to be referred to a specialist and your request will generally be granted. Specialists, reasonably enough, do charge enhanced fees, but if your pet is insured for veterinary fees, the cost to you is eased considerably. Check that you have up-to-date pet health insurance to cover these eventualities.

BEHAVIOUR AND TRAINING

Whether you have acquired a puppy or an adult rescue dog, he has to learn some important lessons if he is to settle in to his new home and to become a much-loved member of your family. However, like people, all dogs are individuals and some learn more quickly than others. Your dog will have to be house-trained and learn to respond to your voice and your commands.

HOUSE-TRAINING A PUPPY

Everyone wants their new dog or puppy to be clean in the house as soon as possible. This is a reasonable ambition, but house-training is not always easy, nor is it necessarily learnt as quickly as we would like. Individual dogs learn at a different pace, and quite often their early background will influence their aptitude to learn as we wish them to do.

◆ Some of the set-backs in house-training will be the fault of the new owner who may not be paying attention to the puppy's needs. House-training is time-consuming and you will need maximum tolerance and patience but, in the end,

ninety-nine per cent of all dogs do reach the stage of absolutely reliable perfection in their house manners.

◆ House-training depends largely on the owner's vigilance, and the crucial factor is to have someone paying attention to the puppy at the moment when he needs to urinate. Young puppies have very little time between realising that they need to urinate and actually doing so. This can also be true of some adult dogs, especially when they have been kennelled and have become used to passing urine at any time. Elderly dogs may also have a very short waiting ability or may even be slightly incontinent, leaking small amounts of urine in an involuntary manner.

◆ Some owners have found that it suits them best to take the puppy outside to pass urine every hour on the hour throughout the day. This is effective, especially with slightly older puppies of twelve weeks or more.

◆ The eight-week-old puppy passes urine more often than once an hour when he is playing, but then he may sleep through the next scheduled hourly exit to the

Above: young puppies, such as this Labrador-cross, are very inquisitive and love to explore their surroundings.

garden, and it would be a pity to wake him when everything is so peaceful. So you must learn to read your puppy and recognise the actions he makes when the urge to urinate comes upon him. Usually, he will break off from his game, sniff around urgently on the floor and then squat down.

◆ You must pay attention and whisk the puppy outside so that you can put him down on the spot you mean him to use, meanwhile saying the magic phrase on which you have decided. House-training always involves taking the puppy outside and staying with him until the desired results are achieved.

◆ Putting the puppy outside the door on his own is worse than useless as he will start to play a game or will just sit at the door crying to come in, whereupon he will wet your carpet once again. You must be outside with him, walking slowly and encouraging him with your special phrase.

◆ If you get the desired results, be lavish with your praise and sometimes reward him with a titbit. If you do not get results, no congratulations are due. You must take the puppy outside again quite soon, and go through the whole process again.

PUNISHMENT

An important lesson for the new owner is that punishment does not help when there is a lapse in house-training and a mess is found indoors. Punishing a puppy for defaecating or urinating indoors just sets back your whole house-training programme and may make the puppy afraid to pass faeces even if the need is urgent.

Of course, you must not punish the puppy if he has diarrhoea overnight and then you come down to a less than flower-fresh kitchen. You may do a bit of under-the-breath grumbling as you clear up, to show that this behaviour is not desirable, but nothing more than that. Your resolution should be to keep a closer watch on the puppy, or to leave him for less time.

◆ The alternative, if you really cannot cope with the outdoor excursions, is to make a thick pad of newspaper in the kitchen or another easily-cleaned room and to put the puppy there when he shows his intentions. Eventually, when he is a little older, you can move some sheets of used newspaper out into the garden and show the puppy where you wish him to go.

◆ Faeces are always passed directly after eating, both in puppies and adults. As soon as the dog's head comes up from an empty feeding bowl, say 'Outside' and then out you both go until the puppy has performed. This same toileting drill can be continued into the dog's old age, and it is especially useful if you and your pet are away from home.

◆ You can help to keep your house clean by not letting the puppy run through all the rooms; keep him in the utility part of the house until house-training is perfected.

◆ You will be surprised at how quickly your puppy associates going outside with urination. You will be delighted the first time that he asks to go out without any prompting from you.

◆ When the house is soiled it will usually be close to the exit door, so always take the puppy out by the same door, and thereby help him to form a habit.

◆ At first you will have to carry the puppy but, as soon as it is practical, make him walk alongside you and wait while you open the door.

HOUSE-TRAINING AN ADULT MONGREL

If your puppy defecates indoors when he has had a few weeks of house-training, you can be sure it is a case of 'gotta-go'. However, what about your adult pet who has been in kennels for a long time? You will need equal patience here, but you can growl louder when the dog behaves as if he was still in kennels.

◆ He must learn to respect your house,

but try to use a jolly voice after the reprimanding growl and suggest that you both go outside for a few minutes. Praise him lavishly when he gets it right.

◆ Male dogs need to mark their territory, and this applies just as much to the neutered dog as the non-neutered one. You may find that when your adult does go outside he prefers to water a favourite shrub, usually a conifer. It is best to leave this shrub in position even after it dies, because the marking point will be used again and again – every time the dog wants to emphasise his ownership.

◆ Be very careful not to punish the adult dog for misbehaving during house-training; it is important to you that you bond with the dog and come to trust each other. Although you may feel that the dog should have known better, it can take a long time for a dog taken out of a rescue kennel situation to realise that life is going to be different now.

Note: never ever, no matter what your elderly relatives say, descend to the ugly and undignified action of 'rubbing his nose in it'. All this achieves is a dog with a smelly face and probably a simmering dislike of being handled by or even approached by his new owner. If your adult dog finds it easy to bark, you may

Below: keep your dog on a lead and under your control, especially when meeting other dogs.

want to encourage him to ask to go out; some dogs find it easy, whereas others never get the message and you have to think for them.

STAYING CLEAN OVERNIGHT

Teaching a puppy to stay clean overnight depends very much on the length of the owner's nights, and the level of noise outside. If the puppy sleeps in a box or a crate in your bedroom, you will be able to respond immediately if he stirs and needs to urinate. If the puppy is left in the kitchen, he will realise his needs at first light, or when the world around him begins to make noises. The sounds of milk or newspapers being delivered, or other animals being put out in gardens will awaken the inquisitive and eager pup, and whoosh goes the urination impulse. Can you get up earlier than the paper boy seven days a week?

As you will conclude from all this,

CLEANING UP

There are many floor and carpet cleaners that you can use to clean up your dog's mess. The important thing is never to use anything containing ammonia, because that will compound the smell of urine so that the same spot will be used again. Disinfectant is useless on a soiled surface, so always wash well with some water and detergent first. Clean up thoroughly as any residual smell may trigger off repeat incidents. Odour eliminator sprays are available from your vet.

gold-standard house-training may take a variable time to teach. About six months is a fair time scale, but never forget that the human baby takes about four times as long.

COMMUNICATING WITH YOUR DOG

It is important to train your puppy or your adult dog to respond to his own name as soon as possible. If you have not yet decided on a name, you can always use the word 'Puppy'. This name will stand as an alternative all the dog's life, and will sometimes serve to jerk the dog's memory when he is determined to ignore his given name. An adult dog will probably have been named in the rescue kennel, and it is a good idea to choose a name that sounds similar because a rescue mongrel may have had several different names before he came to you. Use the puppy's name at every opportunity, prefacing every command with his name.

OTHER VOCABULARY

After the puppy's name, 'No' should be the most important word in his vocabulary. I believe in saying 'No' to things that are definitely not permissible from the very first day that the puppy is in your home. If you saw the puppies with their dam, you may have observed that when they are tormenting the bitch, taking her food, or pushing her off the blanket, she will give a low growl and then if a pup persists, she will make one quick, loud snap close to him but not actually biting. The snap is always made while the offence is being committed, and we know for sure that delayed admonition is always quite useless.

You must catch the puppy, or the dog for that matter, in the act of doing something wrong. One sharp slap administered while the puppy is doing something of which you disapprove, is quite legitimate correction which may on occasion save him from hurt or danger. However, prolonged beating and loss of temper are never acceptable and will merely degrade the human who inflicts it. They do not teach a kindly dog anything beyond making him apprehensive of the owner who behaves in that way. A sharper dog may retaliate by becoming aggressive to people, even to those not guilty of punishing him. If you notice the dog misbehaving and you are some distance away, a small bean bag or a tie filled with pebbles can be thrown on the ground near the dog but not actually on him.

The startling clatter is enough to deter a dog from the action on which he is intent, and, if done consistently, he will soon learn not to act in this way.

TRAINING YOUR DOG

Train your dog or puppy to come to your call. Always use a happy voice and make coming to you worthwhile from the dog's point of view. You could try offering him a titbit, a cuddle or a little game.

◆ Dogs do what pays them best; if you are more fun than chewing the hosepipe, your dog will come to you – it's as simple as that. A food reward usually produces the desired result, but make it a tiny piece of biscuit or a scrap of cheese, not chocolate which is unsuitable for dogs.

◆ Try not to shout at your dog; save your powerful voice for extreme situations. The dog who is constantly shouted at tends to take no notice at all, possibly thinking it is the normal human voice.

◆ In the beginning, the dog has to be eager to come to you. Later on, habit will take over and a reward, beyond a pat and a smile, may not always be necessary.

◆ Call the puppy, always saying his name. You should even use his name when he is coming towards you anyway.

◆ Learn to read each other's facial expressions and body language. The dog will certainly learn about you, to such an extent that he will appear to read your mind before you have even made it up. Our dogs watch us constantly; they read gestures we did not even know we were making. Your facial expressions are important – making eye contact and smiling, even if you do not speak, makes your dog aware that all is right in both your worlds.

Below: whenever your dog responds correctly in training, reward him with a titbit or a pat or cuddle.

SHORT DAILY SESSIONS

Experienced dog trainers believe in short training sessions disguised as dog/human interaction or play. You should try to spend five minutes on dog education, say, three times a day, repeating what the dog was learning before, until marrying up an action with the sounds that you make becomes an automatic reaction in your dog. Remember that your language is just 'sound' to the dog.

Before feeding the dog is usually a useful time to go through an 'obedience' routine because then the dog's attention will be concentrated upon you. You should only elaborate on the basic training and introduce more advanced training when you feel that your dog is ready for it.

◆ Your dog may learn to tease you, to come within arm's length and then dodge away again. It is maddening, and the way to end up winning this game is to turn round and walk away quickly if you are in a place where it is safe to do so. You will soon find your dog close behind you. If the dodging tactic persists, especially when you are in an open space, it may be because you have called the dog to you to put his lead on, thereby effectively ending all his fun.

◆ Practise calling the dog back for a pat and a praise session and then letting him go again. If this does not work, he must be put on a very long rope, which trails behind him. When he will not come to your call, tread on the end of the rope and haul him in, rewarding him when he arrives, even if his intentions were quite different.

Right: your dog will want to please you, but many independent terrier-type mongrels may not always obey you!

'SIT'

This command is a useful 'slower up' of
dog exuberance. 'Sit' is taught by saying
the word when the puppy or dog is going
to sit anyway. Watch your dog closely
when you see him going into the 'sit'
position, then praise him and give a
reward. The dog will soon learn that
folding his back legs under him pays him
well, especially when you are making that .
hissing sound 'Sssitt!' Sometimes you will

need to reinforce the sitting action by
putting light pressure on the dog's back.
Be as consistent as you can. Use your
hands as well as your voice and repeat
the exercise often.

'DOWN'

◆ Sitting and offering a paw to 'shake
hands' is always endearing behaviour.
Alternatively, you may incorporate the
'down' command by asking the dog to
'sit', lie down, and then stand up again,
just before you put the food bowl down.
◆ Never encourage a dog or puppy to

*Above: whenever you notice that your
dog is going to sit, repeat the word 'Sit',
then praise and reward him with a food
titbit and a cuddle.*

*Above: you should always discourage
your dog from jumping up boisterously
to greet you.*

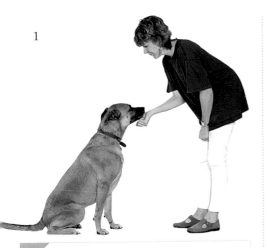

1

To teach 'Down', hold a food titbit in your closed hand and offer it to your dog.

2

Lower your hand to floor level and your dog will follow it until he is lying down to get it out of your hand.

jump up – either at yourself or at visitors and especially not at children. It is better to get down to the dog's level so that he can greet you more easily but this is not always convenient when you or the visitor are wearing your best clothes. Dogs have an inherited instinct to greet people

GREETING ROUTINE

If you want to enjoy your dog to the full you must invent a greeting routine that suits your particular situation, remembering that the dog has been looking forward to this homecoming from the minute after you left. Having something, such as a toy or a glove, to carry in the mouth diffuses an emotional moment.

by licks on the mouth. This is really a throwback to the wild state, when the puppies would lick the bitch's mouth to get her to disgorge partially digested food for them. Indeed, this is still the habit with some young litters and is an action that is combined with the emotion of greeting and pleasure.

◆ Dogs will always delight in your arrival home, and, especially in the excitement of the moment, they can behave more violently than we would like. Provide your dog with some acceptable way to welcome you. Throw a ball and let him bring it back to you – or give him a glove to carry away with great pride and a wagging tail. You could have a routine by which you come in and go straight to the biscuit tin and dispense a treat while the dog is put into the 'sit' position. It does seem a pity to curb your dog's joy and exuberance by reacting with shouting.

'COME'

To teach your dog to come to you on command, he must first learn to 'stay'. Train him gradually over a period of time and always reward him when he does well.

1

1　*Stand close to your dog, then back away slowly, repeating 'Stay'. Gradually increase the distance.*

2

2　*An open-armed welcome encourages him to come back to you.*

3

3　*A little favourite titbit as a reward makes coming back to you worthwhile.*

COLLARS AND LEADS

Put a soft collar on your puppy as soon as you acquire him, and do not forget that he must, by law, wear a dog tag engraved with your home telephone number and address, whenever he is away from home, even in the car. It is as well to let the puppy wear this tag on his collar during his first learning experiences, and then the dangling attachment will always be familiar to him. You can also consider a microchip (see page 53).

If you have obtained an adult dog from a rescue centre, he may already be equipped with a tag giving particulars of the rescue organisation he came from. It is best to remove this tag and substitute one with your own address straight away. Then, if your dog should stray, there is every opportunity for the finder to get in touch directly with you. If a lost dog is taken in by a dog warden and put into the care of kennels, there may be some delay in getting him back and you will have to pay a fee for his recovery and the care he receives.

Train your puppy to wear the soft collar for short periods while he is being supervised. The collar should never be left on when he is alone – tragic injuries have occurred through puppies getting their feet trapped in collars, especially those with elastic inserts, and collars may also get caught on cupboard door handles and similar projections.

LEAD TRAINING

◆ This should begin in the garden and then progress to a quiet road. Begin by putting a light lead on the puppy's collar and walking in the garden slowly, keeping the lead short and the puppy by your side, talking and encouraging all the time. Never use an extending lead or a collar/lead combination for this lesson – a separate collar and a light lead work best.

◆ When the puppy is walking reasonably by your side, progress to training on a pavement, but make the training session your only task at this time. Never try to lead-train when you are on an errand of any kind. Take a few minutes every day to concentrate on your dog, until he is walking at your side,

pulling neither forwards nor backwards.

◆ The concept of 'walking to heel' is inappropriate for a companion dog; keep the dog by your side with no tension on the lead at all. Pulling on the lead gets more difficult to eradicate as the weeks go by, but nothing looks more foolish than an owner being tugged along the road.

◆ Keep the lead short and if the dog pulls forward, turn round and go the other way until the dog is at your side again. You may prevent the dog pulling ahead of you by waving a rolled newspaper in front of his nose but you should never use it to strike the dog. Resist any

Left: a well-trained dog walks quietly at his owner's side, with the owner holding the lead securely across her body in the right hand.

impulse to tug on the dog's neck because this may cause injury to the internal structures of the neck. Persistence, practice and reward will convey your message to the dog, and when you have achieved perfect lead walking you will have taught your dog and, incidentally, yourself something that will serve you both well all of your life together.

Below: 'walking to heel' is not a good idea, especially beside busy roads or on crowded pavements. It can be learnt at obedience classes if you go in for competitions.

CONTROLLING YOUR DOG

Always keep your dog on a short lead in a busy street. Do not let him approach other dogs or people unasked; nor should you allow children to shriek and shout when playing with a puppy. He will become over-excited and may even hurt someone or do some harm to himself in the process.

An adult mongrel from a rescue home needs your very close vigilance for many weeks when he joins your family. You have no way of knowing what the dog's experiences have been and what sounds or incidents may reawaken terror or panic attacks. Sudden sounds or large vehicles passing by in the street, lawn mowers, bicycles, skateboards or even prams may trigger painful memories.

Be ready to cope with the situation and to calm your pet. It follows that the adult rescue dog must not have too much freedom and must never be placed in a situation that may lead to him being frightened. Fear in some dogs shows as an instinct to hide in dark corners or to run away. In others, it may cause a dog to attack. Get to know your adult dog as intimately as possible, as soon as you can.

OTHER COMMANDS

Enjoy playing with your dog, but you must decide when play-time is over. 'That's enough' is a good sound to make to indicate that play must end for now. 'Get in your bed' or 'Into your crate' may be the signal for the dog to retire for a rest.

Some dog trainers recommend putting the toys you play with away in a drawer until you want to play next time. If you do this, make sure that the dog always has a chewing toy of his own – a safe hard rubber toy or a nylon bone is best. Puppies need to chew when they are getting their second set of teeth, a process that begins when they are about four months old and which may continue throughout their first year.

In training your dog, consistency in following a command through is the important keynote. He must always do as you have said, but you must never lose your temper over the encounter. Go on being firm but kind until the dog has given up trying to defy you. Punishment is not appropriate, nor is shouting or violence. Young dogs are not so different from children in their attitudes to rebellion and compliance. Make it worth the dog's while to do as you wish. You should expect, as you would with a child, some attempts to test your firmness and resolution, but do not despair if at times you do not seem to be making a lot of progress.

Right: a playful tussle with a strong adult can be fun but do not encourage your children to do this.

TIME ON THEIR OWN

It does a dog no harm to be ignored for short periods of time when you are busy. Your dog will enjoy your companionship and love the sound of your voice, but he will also need some peace and quiet, and this applies especially to a growing puppy. He should be allowed to sleep until he wakes naturally. When a puppy tires of play and goes into his crate or basket, it is a good idea to leave him alone for a short time, perhaps for ten minutes at first, but extending for up to an hour at ten months old. It is a mistake to let a puppy or an adult dog believe that you are constantly in attendance.

If you start training the puppy to stay alone while you are in another room, you may soon hear the door being scratched and must tell him that such behaviour is not allowed. However, do not be in too much of a hurry to go back to the dog – he will soon learn that he can gain your attention straight away by destroying his surroundings.

When leaving a dog for an hour or two, always tidy the room first. Empty

OTHER ANIMALS

Do not leave your new dog or puppy with an older dog or a resident cat until the older animal has accepted the newcomer on his own terms. Cats should always be provided with a safe and comfortable place high up on top of a cupboard from which they can observe the antics of a puppy without feeling too much aggression.

the waste bin, remove any food; and make sure all the cupboards are securely fastened. Leave some toys in case the dog wakes. Many people leave a radio on, tuned in to a 'talk' programme, so that the sound of human voices provides companionship.

Make your 'goodbyes' very casual. You should not build up an emotional atmosphere between you and the dog – just go. You may want to think out a key phrase for departure, such as 'Be a good dog, look after the house', but it is often better to say nothing at all. If your dog is destructive or barks and howls when you are out, the best strategy is to plan mock departures. Go out and slam the door as if you have really left, and

then observe the dog's behaviour. Tell him off in a severe tone of voice and then depart again, leaving your return a bit longer this time.

SOCIALIZATION

Socialization with all kinds of people and in a wide range of situations is very important in developing a well-balanced companion animal.

◆ If possible, carry your puppy in your arms along a busy road so that he can hear and see traffic noises. Let passers-by talk to the puppy. The prevailing view has always been that puppies should be kept within their own gardens until they have completed the course

PUPPY PARTIES

You may find that your veterinary surgeon runs 'puppy parties' – small gatherings of owners and their new puppies in the area. The puppies are allowed to play together and they are also handled and played with by the other owners, by the veterinary nurses and the vet. This is said to considerably ease visits to the vet in the future as the puppy will always remember the early pleasurable experiences.

of primary vaccinations, probably at three-and-a-half to four months old. The Guide Dogs for the Blind Association have pioneered the system of having puppies vaccinated for the first time at six weeks,

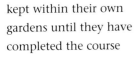

Below: learning to share a toy is a good experience for dogs.

and then allowing them to be taken out and about during the most vital time for learning about the human world, which is between six and twelve weeks of age.

◆ As soon as the puppy or adult dog has complete confidence in your home, invite a range of people in to meet him, such as children, old people, babies in prams, people in wheelchairs, men with beards. They all provide vital experiences for a puppy at his most impressionable age.

Above: get your puppy used to being handled from an early age.

HANDLING THE PUPPY

If you do not have the opportunity to take your puppy to an organised puppy party, at least you can simulate the veterinary examination. Handle your puppy or dog as much as possible. Turn him on to his back and then pick him up; massage his legs; examine his toes; lift up his tail. Do all this gently and with consideration, and praise and reward afterwards, but make it clear that you can do anything reasonable and he must always submit. Establish mutual trust and then gradually extend the privilege to other adult family members.

TRAINING CLASSES

Reinforce the training you have given to your dog by joining a local training class or one that prepares dogs for the Kennel Club Good Citizen Test which covers normal domestic behaviour training of the basic commands: 'Sit', 'Down', 'Stay' and 'Come', etc. Many clubs also run competitive obedience training.

Mongrels are often the stars of agility classes, so if you are fit yourself you may want to join in this cheerful activity. There are many display teams where mongrels are welcome, and where talents can range from absolute precision obedience to being the clown of the party – the one who specializes in doing it wrong! You can do so much more than just own a dog – have fun together and perhaps you will become stars of the canine world.

Above and right: many mongrels enjoy participating in agility classes where they can display their natural talents for jumping.

COMMON BEHAVIOUR PROBLEMS

THE URGE TO WANDER

Probably the predominant problem in mongrel dogs is the inherited tendency to be a free spirit and to wander. The best way to break down this behaviour is to make yourself, your home and garden, the centre of the dog's world, and the place where everything good happens.

Neutering of both sexes undoubtedly helps, removing the sexual urge to seek out random partners.

FEAR BITING AND AGGRESSION

Ideally a dog should not be re-homed from a rescue centre if he shows any signs of fear biting or aggression. Seek advice from the kennel staff. It may be that the problem goes much too deep for amateur retraining and some specialist help may be needed. Although we all want to see every disadvantaged dog make good, we have to accept that some dogs cannot be made safe for life with a human family.

THE ADULT DOG

By the time your puppy grows into an adult, he should be house-trained and obedient. He should respond to your commands, and you should have got to know each other so well that you can both communicate effectively with each other. Your dog will have been assimilated into your home and will have become a much-loved family member and a loyal companion to you.

As well as feeding and exercising your dog on a daily basis, you should groom him regularly, bath him occasionally and keep a sharp eye on his general health to ensure that he stays fit and healthy.

DENTAL CARE

As your puppy comes to the end of his first year, check that all his puppy teeth have been shed, and that the permanent teeth are not coming through on top of the puppy set. Tooth extraction in dogs is relatively easy if your veterinary surgeon advises that this is necessary.

The hard nylabone toys are excellent for keeping the dog's teeth clean, and a hard biscuit as a treat also helps. Your

Above: you should examine your dog's mouth and teeth regularly. Get him accustomed to this from an early age so that he learns to trust your handling him. This will help to make visits to the vet easier when he is older.

veterinary surgeon will advise you if your dog's teeth need cleaning, but mongrel teeth are usually strong and white and it is best to maintain them naturally. Pain in the teeth is often expressed by carrying the ear low on the affected side.

EYES

Always check your dog's eyes frequently, especially if you see any mucous discharge from the corner, if the eyes are held half closed, or the white part of the eye appears bloodshot. Occasionally, grass seeds can be embedded in the eye and will need to be removed professionally.

NAILS

Your dog's nails will generally be worn down by road-walking and exercise on rough land, so they should not require clipping, except in the case of very old dogs. Mongrels often retain their dew claws, a rudimentary nail, semi-circular in shape, which grows roughly at 'wrist level'. If this nail is growing round in a circle and threatens to penetrate the leg, consult your vet who will probably

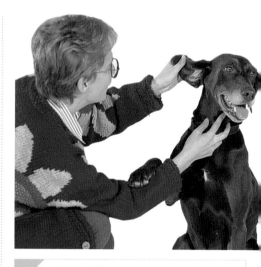

Above: check inside your dog's ears for wax or infestation by parasites.

advise that the whole claw should be removed permanently.

EARS

Ears can get clogged up with dark brown wax, or they may be invaded by parasites. The signs of ear problems are persistent shaking of the head, scratching the ears, holding one lower than the other, and/or a very pungent smell. Take a ball of cotton wool and then gently wipe the ear inside; you may discover that you have removed quite a lot of wax. Never attempt to use a cotton bud or in any way attempt to penetrate the depths of the ear. If the irritation and smell persist, take your dog to the vet for a proper examination of his ears.

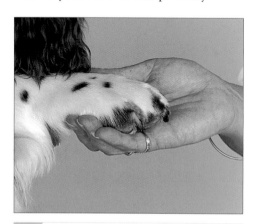

Above: teach your dog to offer his feet to you to be examined.

DIGESTIVE PROBLEMS

Keep a close watch on any episodes of vomiting and diarrhoea. Refusal to eat is unimportant if it lasts only up to forty-eight hours – longer than that requires a professional opinion. Take a sample of the diarrhoea in a small box or pot as it may help the vet in his diagnosis. Do not allow diarrhoea to continue for several days without seeking veterinary advice as it can be a tell-tale sign of many serious medical conditions in a dog.

COUGHING

If your dog's cough sounds as though he has a bone stuck in his throat, it could be kennel cough, an airborne virus which is spread wherever dogs are gathered together and there is one infected dog. Telephone the veterinary surgery to say that you suspect kennel cough. It may be that the vet will make some special arrangements to see you, as no-one wants a coughing dog in the waiting room. Kennel cough can last a very long time so you must be patient and follow the course of treatment. Do not take a coughing dog to a training class, a show or any other canine gathering, and be aware that you can carry the virus on your clothing.

CHOKING

When your dog has a foreign body stuck in his throat, resulting in retching, an

WORMING

Mongrels may need a regular worming routine as it is possible that the puppies may not have been wormed effectively and may carry a persistent burden. Consult the vet where your pet can be weighed and prescribed a worm preparation.

inability to swallow, with drooling and saliva, and possible scratching at his mouth or throat, you must contact your vet urgently (see page 118).

PARASITES

Fleas, lice and ticks are a nuisance to all dogs. Having a dog scratching all the time is not pleasant and may lead to self-inflicted wounds which are difficult to heal. Get a flea eradication remedy from the vet. You need only apply it once in four months for complete freedom from parasites. Ticks are always best removed manually before they become too engorged with blood. Get a nurse at the surgery to show you how to remove a tick and you can then do it for your dog thereafter. Do not neglect ticks – a large number on a small dog could cause anaemia. Ticks are easily picked up in sheep country and in woodlands where there are deer. In fact, it may be possible that deer ticks carry disease.

GROOMING

All dogs need to have dead hair, dust and tangles removed from their coats and no dog can do this for himself. Even if your puppy has a very soft or short-haired coat, get him accustomed to a regular grooming routine from the very beginning. This is another domination routine that is kindly but conveys to the puppy that he has to submit to what you want to do. It is best to groom a small puppy on your lap, but, later on, train your dog to stand on a convenient bench, table or even a garden seat.

SMOOTH-COATED DOGS

◆ Smooth-coated dogs need to have dead hair removed quite frequently and they look all the better for this beauty routine.

◆ Smooth coats are groomed with a hound glove, a kind of mitt with an abrasive surface or wire bristles on one side and a velvet polisher on the other. In fact, you can remove a lot of dead hair just by stroking a smooth coat with a rubber-gloved hand, and then giving it a polish with a piece of pure silk.

◆ Talk to your dog all the time; always remember that the sound of your voice is a pleasure to him, and hand massage is very soothing.

◆ Complete your grooming by looking at the dog's feet. Some dogs seem to resent their feet being touched, so accustom your dog to offering his feet to you willingly. Check that the nails are not over-long; they should just touch the ground when the dog is standing. Some nails may be split or torn, so use nail clippers to take off any ragged pieces and finish by buffing them with an emery board.

LONG-COATED DOGS

◆ Long-coated mongrels require more grooming. Depending on the dog's ancestry, the coat can be difficult to

GROOMING EQUIPMENT

Your local pet shop or vet will advise you on the tools most suited to grooming your dog. A hound glove is ideal for smooth-haired dogs, whereas a more traditional brush and comb probably work better on long-haired dogs.

Note: while you are grooming, always check for any swellings or lumps and report them to the vet. They may be the beginnings of a malignant or benign tumour, so it is best to get any lump diagnosed early.

groom, or relatively easy. Some silky coats tend to clog into tangles very easily. These tangles are often found in the armpits or the groin. They can be quickly teased out but they will very soon matte again. The simplest thing is to clip out these tangles where they do not show.

◆ Go through the rest of the coat with a steel comb, taking out any burrs, leaves and seeds. Surplus hair should be trimmed out from between the pads of the feet, and hair on the top of the feet may be trimmed short to help prevent any mud being brought into the house.

◆ Hair under the tail and on the sheath of the male should be carefully trimmed off to avoid unpleasant smells. Clean around the anus with a pad of damp cotton

wool. Be sure to remove any accumulated faeces as flies may be attracted by any residue on or around the tail.

◆ If you have noticed your dog 'scooting' on his behind, this may be caused by over-full, or even impacted, anal glands – not worms. Take the dog to the vet to have the anal glands emptied.

◆ Give the coat a thorough brushing to get rid of dust and make it shine. Your dog will come to enjoy these grooming sessions.

Left: teach your dog to stand on a table or a bench when you are grooming him.

BATHING YOUR DOG

Dogs should not require bathing very often – a couple of times a year is usually enough unless your dog makes a habit of rolling in unpleasant things. Small dogs are best bathed standing in the kitchen sink, on a pile of towels or a non-slip bath mat to prevent them slipping. However, a larger dog may have to be washed in the shower or outside in the garden in a tub or an old bath.

BATHING TIPS

◆ If you have a dog with many white areas in his coat, you might like to wash the white parts only without bathing the whole dog.

◆ Always use a dog shampoo, which is specially formulated for dogs.

◆ If you suspect that your dog has fleas, stand him on a sheet of white paper and comb the coat thoroughly. A lot of soot-like dust may drop down on to the paper. Pour a few drops of cold water on to this dust; if it turns red, your dog has fleas – the red colouring being the blood on which the fleas have fed. The dog must be bathed in either a good anti-parasitic shampoo or alternative product. The house, most especially the area where the dog lies and his bedding,

should be treated with an appropriate anti-parasitic spray. You can obtain these products from your veterinary surgery.

◆ Put a circle of vaseline around the eye area to prevent soap getting into the eyes.

◆ If you have a light-coloured dog which needs bathing often, it may be a good

idea to accustom him to being dried with a hair dryer. Take care not to have the dryer too hot and to keep it moving around the dog's body, not directing it for too long at any one area.

◆ Always dry the dog thoroughly, either with a hair dryer or by rubbing him well in a clean towel and then allowing him to dry off outside in the sun. Don't allow him to stay damp or to go to sleep in his bed before drying off.

STRIPPING AND TRIMMING YOUR DOG

Mongrels with terrier ancestry are likely to have wiry coats, which will require regular stripping to remove dead hair. Ask a terrier owner to show you how to do this with a stripping knife – a purpose-made tool with serrated edges. Alternatively, you may choose to have your dog professionally trimmed about twice a year.

DEAD HAIR AND MOULTING

Really dense-coated Chow-Chow or Spitz-type dogs need regular brushing, first the 'wrong way' against the hair growth and then again to bring the hair back into place. Periodically these breeds, as well as Labrador and Old English Sheepdog crosses, will have a huge seasonal moult, losing great quantities of their undercoat and top coat.

Take your dog into the garden and remove as much dead hair as possible.

EXERCISE

All dogs need a certain amount of exercise but no dog would vote for long walks on a lead beside busy roads. Exercise, from the dog's point of view, is about developing and maintaining bodily skills, but it is also the equivalent of reading the local newspapers to find out what is going on and who or what is in the neighbourhood. Giving a dog a free run off the lead stimulates his very powerful sense of smell and his ability to identify and track other creatures.

However, to many owners giving their dog free exercise can only happen when there is time to drive to a suitable open space. Letting a dog run free in an urban situation is anti-social behaviour for a wide range of reasons, including the danger from traffic, bicycles and pedestrians. Find out if there is a park or some open heathland near your home where your dog can run freely and safely off the lead.

Below: sticks of this kind can break easily and can be dangerous. A sturdy rubber toy is safer and more fun.

We should separate in our minds the provision of exercise and play for the dog, and the opportunity to defaecate and urinate. These are necessary functions which can be, and should be, performed in your own garden where you have the opportunity to clear up properly. This routine is easy to train for, as it is just a progression from the puppy house-training method. 'Doing it at home' is useful in many ways, especially if the dog or his owner is sick, or when the dog is elderly and cannot walk far, or the weather is bad.

PLAYTIME

Playing daily with your dog is equally important. Not only is it another means of exercising him but also a way of developing his mental skills and his bonding with the human family. Play is part of the fun of owning a dog, and it can take many forms. Indoor play focuses on 'seek and find' skills, or catching a suitable toy or tugging on a rope. You can

reinforce your essential dominance by requiring the dog to give the toy to you – or perhaps by refusing to play at the actual moment when the dog requests your attention. If you play these games, make sure that you are always the winner, and call a halt to them by saying your keynote word or phrase, such as 'that's enough'.

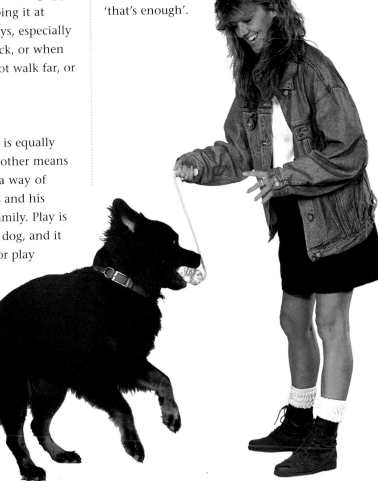

Right: catching a moving object is one of the natural canine skills.

TRAVELLING AND HOLIDAYS

You probably brought your new dog or puppy home in a car. This first journey is usually made with the dog being held securely on someone's lap but on subsequent journeys you should take measures to ensure your dog's safety.

CAR TRAVEL

Almost all dogs are carsick at first. The simplest way to get over this is to ignore the drooling and discomfort and clean up as best you can. Protect the upholstery as much as possible, and take the dog for several short journeys just to get him accustomed to riding in the car. Pick a time before he is fed. It is rare for car sickness to persist, and when it does, it is probably because lots of remedies have been tried and an atmosphere of tension persists when a car ride is inevitable.

◆ The dog wants to be with you all the time and he will willingly jump into the car when you go out. Dogs have an excellent sense of balance so they have a natural ability to ride the roads.

◆ There are many accessories for canine car travel now available to make travelling safer for both the dog and the driver. An adaptation of the wire crate, which you use at home, can partition off the back of the car. Otherwise, there are canine seat belts on sale which will secure the dog on the back seat. It hardly needs to be said that dogs never travel in the front of the car once their baby puppy days are over.

◆ Never forget your dog's comfort in the car. Always carry some water and a bowl, and, in extremely hot weather, a sponge and wet towel are a practical way to cool down a dog which has become overheated.

◆ Never leave a dog in a car, even in slightly warm weather – carry a

Left: many people enjoy going away on holiday with their dog.

thermometer in the car and just see how it heats up! Leaving windows open is of very little use as there is no current of air to cool the dog. A car very quickly becomes an oven, and every year some dogs die a cruel death through suffocation.

HOLIDAYS

Because your dog is part of your family, you will want to include him in your days out and your holidays. There are still some places where your dog will be welcome, but the number is dwindling because of some owners' carelessness and their thoughtlessness in allowing their dogs to damage and soil other people's property.

When you discover some holiday accommodation that permits and welcomes dogs, it is useful to inquire in advance just what facilities will be available to you. Some hotels allow dogs into their grounds but require them to sleep in kennels, or in the owner's car overnight.

The general and understandable rule is that dogs are not permitted in restaurants or public rooms, and often not in the bars of inns where food is served. Take care that what your dog does is not the excuse for banning dogs for ever from that particular establishment.

Many camping sites or caravan parks require dogs to be tied up outside their owner's van. This is the way to bring out the worst behaviour in any dog, such as persistent barking, threatening people who

THE COUNTRY CODE

When out in the countryside, always keep your dog on a lead when you are near livestock. Even if he behaves impeccably, it is possible that cattle, sheep and poultry may panic at the mere sight of him. Take special care to keep him on a lead when there are deer around – few dogs can resist the chase. All the training and domestication we can give is only a thin veneer over the basic wild dog. Think ahead for your pet and keep him out of trouble.

approach too closely and, almost inevitably, plotting every chance to escape – not much of a holiday for the dog or his owner.

TRAVELLING AND QUARANTINE

Dogs travel free of charge on most trains, but keep them off the seats! Long-distance coaches do not carry dogs. As regulations stand now, pets can be taken freely to Europe but they cannot come back into Britain without undergoing six months in quarantine kennels. Dogs may travel by air or sea to the Channel Islands, the Isle of Man, and to Northern Ireland or Eire without being subjected to quarantine on their return.

Most internal and external airlines require that dogs travel as freight in special secure containers which can be hired from the airline. The only exceptions are very small dogs which may be allowed to travel in the cabin with their owner.

BOARDING KENNELS

It is not a bad thing to accustom your dog to going into a boarding kennel for one or two nights while he is still a puppy. Some dogs dislike the noise of kennels, and it is up to you to know your dog so well that you will be aware if he is noise-sensitive.

Boarding kennels usually charge you by the day and have strict rules about the times during which dogs can be delivered and collected. The best kennels get booked up very early for popular holiday periods so make arrangements for your dog

as soon as you know you are going away. Be sure to ask which vaccinations are necessary and get them done at least two weeks before the dog goes into kennels. **Note:** if your dog came from a rescue kennel, you may find that they also take holiday boarders.

THE ELDERLY DOG

Mongrel owners are so fortunate – their dogs usually live longer than some of their pedigree cousins. However, even the mongrel eventually shows the inevitable signs of the ageing process. So much more can be done for our dogs nowadays, so do not despair if your dog shows signs of illness.

◆ Lameness and pain on getting up from his bed are among the earliest signs that your dog has arthritis, a condition that is excruciatingly painful although movement sometimes eases the pain. There are medical treatments and even hip joint replacements, so consult your veterinary surgeon.

◆ Elderly dogs may become partially or completely blind. They can manage extremely well in a familiar environment provided that all the furniture is kept in the same place. You will have to think ahead for your dog and protect him from any hazards.

◆ The same is true for the old dog who becomes deaf. Hand signals are helpful as is your continual watchfulness, especially when any household appliances are being used.

◆ Old dogs frequently seem confused when they wake from sleep; they appear not to know quite where they are. When outside, even in your own garden, the geriatric dog may move off surprisingly quickly albeit in completely the wrong direction.

◆ Care and consideration must be your watchwords. Elderly dogs appear to vary in health and capability from day to day. An ageing digestion may appreciate smaller, easily digested meals given more frequently, say, four times a day. When the teeth are no longer comfortable, soft food is easier for the dog to eat. Special treats, praise and affection can mean so much to both of you when your pet is approaching the end of his days.

◆ Incontinence can be a problem in old age, especially in spayed bitches. Once more, your vet can help with medical treatment, and you can also save yourself trouble by protecting the dog's bed with a waterproof surface placed under a polyester fur rug.

◆ Best of all, old dogs love a beanbag to support their weary limbs. Smooth-coated dogs will be comforted by a coat to cover the chest and haunches, and in draughty old houses, the coat may be necessary, even indoors; but take it off as often as

you can to allow air to the skin.

◆ Keep your elderly pet clean by wiping his mouth, face and whiskers after eating, and removing any mucous from the eyes with damp cotton wool. Never hesitate to consult your vet about any of your dog's disabilities. The fear that you will be told that putting him to sleep is the answer should be banished from your mind because it is no longer true. Veterinary surgeons are very skilled and are eager to keep an enduring pet relationship going as long as both the owner and dog benefit and are happy in company.

HEALTH AND FIRST AID

SIGNS OF A HEALTHY DOG

A happy, healthy dog wags his tail and is always pleased to see you.
- He is bright and full of bounce.
- He has a good appetite.
- He is eager to go for a walk and does not limp.
- His eyes are bright and free of any discharge.
- His teeth are clean and his breath doesn't smell.
- There should be no discharge from the nostrils. Neither the temperature nor moisture of the tip of the nose are reliable indicators of health in a dog.
- The ears should have only a trace of wax, should not smell and should be pain-free.
- He should breathe through the nose when resting; through the mouth when excited or hot.
- He scratches occasionally, but not persistently.
- He produces a solid motion (with no traces of mucus or blood) once or twice a day.
- He has no discharges or unpleasant smells from the anus or genitals.

DIET

Dogs need a number of basic ingredients in their diet:
- **Protein** from meat, fish, eggs or milk for growth and repair of body tissues.
- **Carbohydrate** from cereal starches and root vegetables for energy and heat.
- **Fat** from dairy produce, meat and oils for energy, palatability and fat-soluble vitamins.
- **Water, vitamins and minerals.**

It is not easy to put together a satisfactory diet at home, as all these elements need to be present in the right proportions and correct quantities to take into account the dog's size, age and activity.

For the majority of owners, it is better to feed a pre-prepared diet, of which there is a bewildering variety available in pet shops and supermarkets, including:
- Canned plus biscuit
- Semi-moist
- Complete dry
- Frozen

The best advice on how to select a particular brand is to choose one recommended for your type of dog and his age which suits your dog, is palatable and does not cause digestive upset or any

SPECIAL DIETS

A number of manufacturers now make special diets for the various stages of a dog's life, to take account of their changing nutritional requirements. These include the following:

◆ Puppies from weaning to four months who should be fed four meals per day.

◆ Puppies from four to five months who need three meals per day.

◆ Puppies from five to six months on two meals per day.

◆ Puppies and adults from six months onwards on one or two meals a day.

◆ Growing, working, pregnant or lactating dogs who need to eat more than normal adults.

◆ Older dogs who generally need less protein.

◆ Overweight dogs who need fewer calories.

◆ Sick dogs with special dietary needs.
Note: take advice from your vet if your dog falls into any of these categories.

other health problems, fits your budget and is regularly available locally.

◆ PRESCRIPTION DIETS

There is also an increasing range of diets available on veterinary prescription for the treatment and management of certain diseases, such as heart disease, kidney or liver failure and allergies.

◆ SCRAPS AND SUPPLEMENTS

Table scraps may be added, so long as they make up no more than between ten and twenty per cent of the dog's total diet. Vitamin and mineral supplements are not normally necessary when feeding a proprietary dog food except during pregnancy and lactation, and should not be given except on veterinary advice.

◆ BONES

Dogs often enjoy chewing bones, and although these may keep them occupied for some time, they can also cause problems, such as broken teeth, choking or bowel obstructions. There are many different types of dog chews on the market which are far more trouble-free, and should be given in preference to bones.

EXERCISE

All dogs need exercise, but how much and how often depends on the size and build of your dog. He needs to be let out to urinate and defecate, to exercise his muscles, to meet and play with other dogs and to alleviate boredom. Walking on the lead is good discipline, but free exercise in a safe area is essential. Teach your dog to play with toys, such as ropes, balls, frisbees and tugs.

You should limit the exercise for your dog if he has breathing problems, a heart condition, is lame, has had a recent injury, or has a digestive upset. When the weather is hot, go out early in the morning or wait until evening to avoid the possibility of heat stroke (see First Aid, page 122).

DAILY CARE

As part of the daily care of your dog, you should briefly check the following.

◆ TEETH

Regular tooth brushing, using a special dog toothbrush or a child's brush and a dog toothpaste (special flavours – they don't like mint!) will discourage the build up of deposits of calculus on the teeth, keeping the dog's teeth healthy and his breath fresh. Start gently to get him used to the idea; handle his mouth, lift his lips and run your finger along the outside of his teeth. Once he is used to this, slowly insert the brush along the side of the mouth, and gently brush up and down and along the teeth. You can always ask your vet for a dental check up just to make sure that everything is in order.

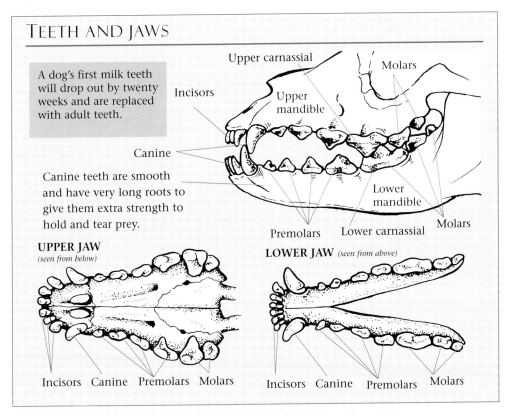

TEETH AND JAWS

A dog's first milk teeth will drop out by twenty weeks and are replaced with adult teeth.

Canine teeth are smooth and have very long roots to give them extra strength to hold and tear prey.

Upper carnassial

Molars

Incisors

Upper mandible

Canine

Lower mandible

Premolars   Lower carnassial   Molars

UPPER JAW *(seen from below)*

Incisors   Canine   Premolars   Molars

LOWER JAW *(seen from above)*

Incisors   Canine   Premolars   Molars

◆ EYES

These should be bright and clear, with no sign of discharge in the corners. You can check your dog's vision by throwing a small titbit for him, and noting whether he is able to follow it. The cornea should be clear, not cloudy and the third eyelid well down in the corner. Both eyes should be open the same amount and appear the same size: any difference may be due to pain or disease, and should be checked.

◆ EARS

Normal ears have just a trace of light brown wax, and very little smell. If your dog's ears are excessively hairy, this may encourage the build up of wax, and reduce healthy air circulation to the ear canal, so keep the hair well trimmed. A powerful smell, discharge, scratching at the ears, or pain on touching them are all signs of ear infection, and should be dealt with immediately by your vet.

◆ NOSE

There are many theories about whether dogs' noses should be warm, cool, moist or dry, but these are not reliable indicators of health or disease. Normal noses simply do vary a lot. What you are looking out

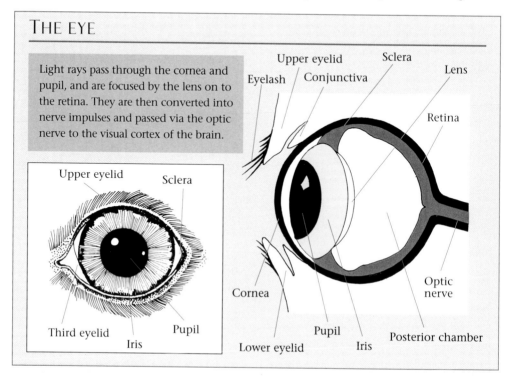

THE EYE

Light rays pass through the cornea and pupil, and are focused by the lens on to the retina. They are then converted into nerve impulses and passed via the optic nerve to the visual cortex of the brain.

Upper eyelid   Sclera
Eyelash   Conjunctiva   Lens
Retina
Upper eyelid   Sclera
Third eyelid   Pupil   Iris
Cornea
Optic nerve
Pupil   Iris   Posterior chamber
Lower eyelid

for are any signs of a discharge, any change in shape, colour, sneezing, ulcers or thickening of the nasal pad.

◆ FEET

'Lame is pain', so any limping should, of course, be investigated by your vet, but a good daily check at home is a sensible routine, particularly if your dog is sensitive about having his feet touched. Make a game of it until he doesn't mind any more. Check the length of his nails and the skin between the pads; it should be pale pink, with no redness or swellings. Long-haired dogs benefit from having the hair between the toes and pads trimmed short; this prevents mattes forming and discourages grass seeds from working their way into the skin of the foot.

◆ URINE AND FAECES

There is no need to become obsessed here, but just check now and again on the frequency of defaecation, that the faeces are of firm, even consistency and dark brown in colour, with no signs of mucus, blood or foreign material, such as cloth or plastic. If your dog has any diarrhoea, it is better to call the vet for advice. Dogs vary enormously in the number of times they stop to pass urine; very frequent urination may just be territory marking. The urine should be pale yellow. If you see your dog trying to urinate, but without success – staying in

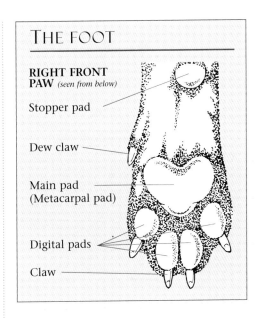

THE FOOT

RIGHT FRONT PAW *(seen from below)*

Stopper pad

Dew claw

Main pad
(Metacarpal pad)

Digital pads

Claw

position but not producing anything – ask your vet to have a look.

◆ GROOMING

Regular combing with a metal comb, or brushing, helps remove any loose dead hair, and prevents mattes forming. Wiry coats benefit from stripping out every three to four months, and curly-coated dogs may need to be clipped to prevent the coat from growing too long.

A very fine-toothed metal comb will pick up any fleas or flea dirts (small brown flakes), and so tell you when you need to repeat any flea treatments. Dogs may be bathed, but only use a mild dog shampoo and follow veterinary advice so as not to dry out the coat and skin.

PERIODIC HEALTH CARE

◆ VACCINATION

Dogs can now be vaccinated against many of the important infectious diseases: distemper, adenovirus 1 and 2, leptospirosis and parvovirus. Puppies should be vaccinated for the first time at eight to nine weeks old or as advised by your veterinary surgeon who knows the local risks, with a second injection at around twelve weeks, and then yearly boosters thereafter.
Note: a kennel cough vaccine is also available, giving good protection within five days. It lasts for six to ten months.

◆ WORMING

All puppies are born infected with roundworms, and can pick up further

infections from their environment in their first three months of life. Faeces from puppies less than six months old and from pregnant bitches or those around the time of their season should be picked up and disposed of, as they are likely to contain worm eggs. After two to three weeks outside the dog, these eggs become infective, both for dogs and children (see Zoonoses, page 107).
◆ Worm all puppies fortnightly from two weeks old up until twelve weeks of age.
◆ Worm all adult dogs at least twice yearly and during pregnancy.
◆ Tapeworms cannot be passed directly from dog to dog in one species: the flea is part of its life cycle. All dogs should be treated for tapeworms at least twice yearly.
◆ Signs of worm infestation include licking at the anus, occasional diarrhoea and weight loss, and pot belly in puppies.

◆ NEUTERING, STERILIZATION, SPAYING AND CASTRATION

These are very much routine operations for your local veterinary clinic, but will probably involve a day's hospitalization. Dogs are usually neutered when they are physically mature, typically from six months onwards.
◆ **For female dogs** the standard neutering operation is an ovariohysterectomy, usually carried out after the first season. This involves removing both the ovaries and the body of the uterus or womb. It

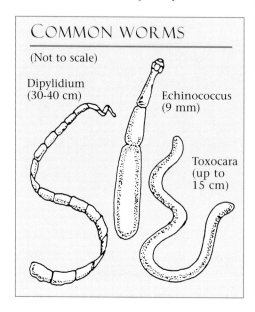

COMMON WORMS

(Not to scale)

Dipylidium
(30-40 cm)

Echinococcus
(9 mm)

Toxocara
(up to
15 cm)

therefore will prevent a bitch from coming into season again, thus stopping all the unwanted attentions of local male dogs, avoiding the problems of bleeding from the vulva during the season, and preventing any possibility of future pregnancies or the development of a womb infection – pyometra – in later life. It also dramatically reduces the likelihood of your dog developing mammary cancer.

Hormonal control of your bitch's seasons is also possible, but not without side effects, and the long-term expense can be considerable. Check your dog's mammary glands after each season for signs of milk production or any swellings.

◆ **In male dogs**, castration involves the complete removal of both testicles. These are the main source of male sex hormones, so castration of a younger dog is likely to reduce his desire to stray or wander off in search of bitches in season, and may help to control his 'mounting', territory marking with urine or any aggressive behaviour he may develop. Certain diseases, e.g. cancer of the prostate gland or hormonally controlled tumours, may also benefit from castration.

◆ **FLEA CONTROL**

The main source of new flea infestation for dogs is from fleas newly hatched from the breeding grounds in your house, not from other animals. Adult fleas spend their entire three-week life on an animal,

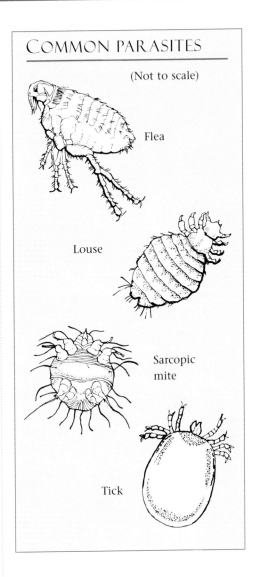

COMMON PARASITES

(Not to scale)

Flea

Louse

Sarcopic mite

Tick

feeding on their blood. Each adult flea lays around twenty eggs a day: these 400 flea eggs drop off the animal onto the dog's bedding or a domestic carpet, and, after hatching, develop into larvae and

INSURANCE

Many insurance companies offer pet health insurance schemes. Taking out an insurance policy means that you can afford the best veterinary care, should your dog need it. Ask for details at your veterinary surgery.

then pupae and, finally, more adults, who each may lay up to 400 more eggs. The whole process may take a few weeks or as long as a year.

In order to have effective flea control on your dog, it is very important to stop the build up of a developing flea population in your house. There are three main types of flea control:

1 External treatment for the dog that kills adult fleas currently present (sprays, powders, shampoos, drops for the coat).

2 Treatment for the home environment that kills developing fleas (mostly sprays).

3 A prescription medicine, available only from your veterinary surgeon, given to your dog in his food each month, which stops the fleas from reproducing.

◆ IDENTIFICATION

It is a legal necessity for your dog to wear a collar and external identification, such as an engraved disc or dog tag, whenever he goes out, so make sure that he always wears his. It is now possible to have a small microchip with the dog's identification number on it placed under his skin – this is relatively painless and can be done while you wait at the vet's surgery. A microchip reader, as used by dog wardens, veterinary surgeries and rescue centres all over the country, will rapidly identify your dog and allow you to be reunited should he ever get lost!

◆ NAIL CLIPPING

Regular exercise on a hard surface, such as pavements and hard ground, will normally keep your dog's nails at the correct length. Check regularly for over-growth and for any signs of discharge around the base of the nail. Trim nails where necessary, avoiding the sensitive tissue (the quick). Ask your vet for guidance on this.

MONGRELS' SPECIAL HEALTH PROBLEMS

Mongrel dogs are the product of a mix of genetic material. They are not predisposed to the wide range of inherited and congenital problems that plague many pedigree breeds which have been selected for their looks or specific aspects of their performance. However, mongrels are susceptible to infectious disease and to the ageing process.

DISEASES AND ILLNESSES

RESPIRATORY DISEASES

When a dog breathes in, air containing oxygen is drawn through the nose or mouth, down the windpipe (trachea) and into the lungs through the bronchi. Relaxation of the breathing muscles pushes the waste air back out again.

◆ SIGNS AND CAUSES

The main signs of respiratory disease are coughing, difficulty in breathing, nasal discharge or sneezing, due to infection, inflammation and irritation or an accumulation of fluid or discharges in the respiratory system. Inflammation of the lung tissue is called pneumonia; in the bronchial tubes (bronchitis); the windpipe (tracheitis); or in the nose (rhinitis).

Respiratory disease may be caused by bacterial, viral or parasitic infections, heart or circulatory system disease, or allergies, and certain types of cancer may spread (metastasize) from a primary site elsewhere to the lungs. Inhalation of food or other foreign material, build up of fluid around the lungs, excessive heat or the malfunctioning of the larynx or trachea may also cause signs of respiratory disease.

Your vet will first examine your dog's respiratory system using a stethoscope,

THE RESPIRATORY SYSTEM

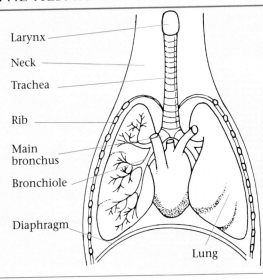

Larynx

Neck

Trachea

Rib

Main bronchus

Bronchiole

Diaphragm

Lung

The larynx, trachea, lungs and bronchi, together with the nose, make up the dog's respiratory system. Air is inhaled through the nose, filtered and passed through the larynx into the trachea. It enters the lungs through the bronchi, which subdivide into bronchioles and end in alveoli, or air sacs. Oxygen and carbon dioxide gases are exchanged in the alveoli.

and then may want to take chest X-rays, use an endoscope to look down the dog's windpipe, or take some samples of the discharges for laboratory analysis.

◆ **KENNEL COUGH**

(See Infectious Diseases, below.)

◆ **CARDIAC COUGH**

(See Heart and Circulation, opposite.)

INFECTIOUS DISEASES

◆ **PARVOVIRUS**

This is a very contagious virus infection, causing heart muscle disease in puppies, and haemorrhagic gastroenteritis in older dogs. Affected animals can succumb very rapidly, and are in urgent need of veterinary care. All puppies should be vaccinated from eight to nine weeks old.

◆ **DISTEMPER**

This is a virus infection affecting the respiratory, digestive and nervous systems. The incubation period is from two to seven days. Distemper causes a high temperature, nasal and ocular discharges, coughing, vomiting and diarrhoea, progressing to fits and death. Treatment depends on the stage of the disease, and is mainly symptomatic, but it may include broad-spectrum antibiotics and anti-convulsants if the nervous system is involved. Effective vaccines are available.

◆ **VIRUS HEPATITIS**

A serious and highly contagious viral infection, this primarily affects the liver,

with an incubation period of five to fifteen days. It is most common in young dogs. Signs of infection include vomiting, diarrhoea, fever, abdominal pain, prostration and death. These dogs are in urgent need of veterinary care, but treatment is mainly symptomatic, and may not be successful. This disease can be prevented simply by vaccination.

◆ **RESPIRATORY ADENOVIRUS**

This virus infection is related to the Canine Hepatitis Virus. It causes a localized respiratory infection.

◆ **LEPTOSPIROSIS**

This is a bacterial infection carried by rats; it is present in some stagnant ponds. It affects the dog's liver or kidneys. The incubation period is from five to fifteen days. It causes fever, thirst, vomiting, jaundice and diarrhoea, progressing to profound depression and death. Prompt and intensive antibiotic and intravenous fluid treatment can be life saving. This disease is transmissible to humans.

◆ **KENNEL COUGH**

This is a highly contagious mixed bacterial (Bordatella) and viral infection of the upper respiratory system. It has an incubation period of five to ten days. Infection is rarely severe, but may be distressing for the dog and owner. It is generally self-limiting in two to three weeks.

◆ **SALMONELLOSIS**

A relatively rare cause of bacterial enteritis in dogs, this can be a potential hazard to humans in contact (see Zoonoses, below).

◆ CAMPYLOBACTER

This causes a profuse bacterial diarrhoea, and is found in up to ten per cent of dogs with enteritis. It can be contagious to people.

◆ RABIES

This is a virus disease of the central nervous system, spread by saliva (mostly from bites), and affecting all mammals. It is not currently present in the UK. It has a long incubation period of up to ten months, during which time no symptoms are seen, but the virus may be present in the dog's saliva during the last few days or weeks. Marked behavioural changes, either the 'furious' or 'dumb' forms, lead to inevitable death as the brain becomes affected. Modern vaccines provide a good level of protection.

◆ ZOONOSES

Zoonoses are animal diseases which can also be caught by humans. Fortunately these are relatively rare. They include:

◆ **Roundworms** (toxoacara visceral larva migrans), which cause eye problems in about 100 children in the UK each year.

◆ **Ringworm**, a fungal skin infection which may be disfiguring.

◆ **Fleas and ticks**.

◆ **A type of tapeworm** (echinococcus hydatid cysts in the liver or brain).

◆ **Leptospirosis**, a liver and kidney infection.

◆ **Scabies**, an irritant rash caused by the sarcoptes mange mite.

SENSIBLE PRECAUTIONS

◆ Vaccinate your dog against any contagious diseases.
◆ Always wash your hands after handling your dog.
◆ Always use separate food bowls and implements for dogs and people.
◆ Worm your dog at least twice a year.
◆ Clear up your dog's faeces, using a 'poop scoop', both in your garden and in public.
◆ Do not let your dog lick your children's faces.
◆ Wash your dog's bedding frequently.
◆ Routinely treat your dog for fleas and other external parasites.
◆ Have your dog's health regularly checked by your vet.
◆ Keep your dog's tetanus vaccinations up to date.

◆ **Salmonella and campylobacter** (gastroenteritis).

◆ **Giardiasis, tuberculosis, brucellosis, chlamydia, pasteurella, tetanus and allergies.**

HEART AND CIRCULATION DISEASES

Contractions of the heart muscle pump blood through a system of valves, sending it, under pressure, round the body. The blood takes oxygen and nutrients to the body's cells, and carries away their waste products. For the system to work well, the heart muscle has to pump regularly, the valves must not leak, and the blood vessels must remain elastic.

◆ SIGNS OF DISEASE

The signs of the heart or circulatory disease that develops with advancing age – commonly a progressive failure of the valves to close properly or of the muscle to contract efficiently – are weakness and a reduced ability to exercise, breathing difficulty and coughing. Internal bleeding, liver disease, overwhelming infections or tumours can also cause signs of circulatory disease.

◆ DIAGNOSIS

Your vet will initially feel your dog's pulse, then listen to the rhythm and rate of the heart and to the sounds of the heart valves with a stethoscope. More detailed investigation may involve taking X-rays of the chest, taking electrical measurements or an ultrasound scan to see a moving image of the heart.

◆ TREATMENT

Excess fluid build up may be cleared by the use of diuretics, which stimulate fluid loss through the kidneys, and by reducing the sodium (salt) content of the diet. Other drugs modify the heart's output and the blood pressure.

SECTION OF THE HEART

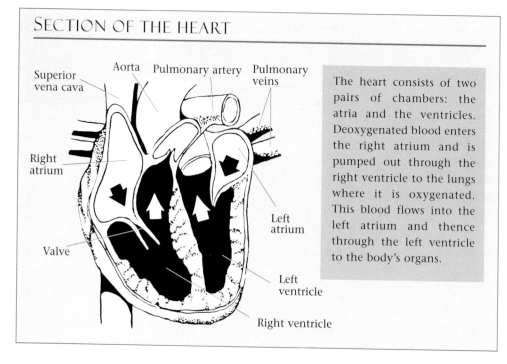

Superior vena cava
Aorta
Pulmonary artery
Pulmonary veins
Right atrium
Valve
Left atrium
Left ventricle
Right ventricle

The heart consists of two pairs of chambers: the atria and the ventricles. Deoxygenated blood enters the right atrium and is pumped out through the right ventricle to the lungs where it is oxygenated. This blood flows into the left atrium and thence through the left ventricle to the body's organs.

THE DIGESTIVE SYSTEM

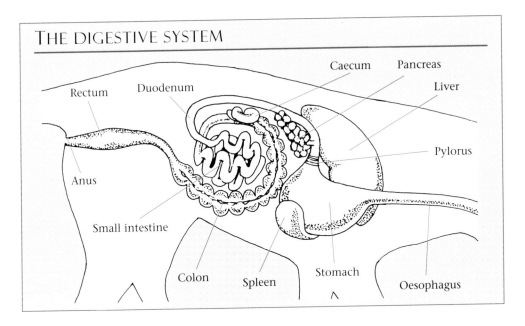

Caecum
Pancreas
Liver
Rectum
Duodenum
Pylorus
Anus
Small intestine
Colon
Spleen
Stomach
Oesophagus

DIGESTIVE SYSTEM DISEASES

The teeth are used to tear and grind food, the stomach further breaks it down, and true digestion takes place in the small intestine. The large intestine is mainly concerned with the reabsorption of fluid, and the rectum stores faeces before they are passed at intervals through the anus.

◆ Digestive system diseases include those of abnormal motility of the gut, abnormal secretion of digestive enzymes, the inflammation of the gut wall and the malfunction of the pancreas and liver.

◆ **SIGNS OF DISEASE**

The signs of disease may include vomiting, diarrhoea or constipation, changes in appetite or weight loss.

◆ **DIAGNOSIS**

Your vet will ask you questions about the frequency, quantity, colour and consistency of any vomit or diarrhoea passed, and about changes in appetite and recent diet, and may need to take a blood or stool sample from your dog.

◆ **TREATMENT**

This may involve changes in diet, or some treatment with antibiotics, anti-inflammatories or drugs that affect the motility of the gut (see Diarrhoea, page 120, Vomiting, page 126).

DENTAL DISEASE

A dog's teeth are used for tearing and chewing food, for biting and, when bared,

SECTION OF A TOOTH

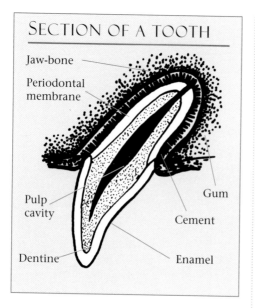

Jaw-bone
Periodontal membrane
Pulp cavity
Dentine
Gum
Cement
Enamel

for signalling aggression. The primary teeth start to fall out at four to five months of age, but they are frequently swallowed, so may not be noticed.

◆ **SIGNS OF DISEASE**
On modern pre-prepared diets, the teeth are often under-used, and large deposits of dental calculus can build up. This may be associated with varying degrees of periodontal disease: bacterial infection, gum recession, salivation, pain, bleeding and halitosis.

◆ **TREATMENT**
This involves breaking off the calculus, polishing the teeth to slow down the deposition of new calculus, and a long-term programme of tooth brushing carried out by the dog's owner at home.

LIVER DISEASES

The liver plays a major role in the metabolism of carbohydrates, proteins, fats and vitamins. It breaks down a wide variety of toxic products in the blood and produces bile (essential for the digestion of fats in the gut).

Liver disease may be rapid in onset (e.g. virus hepatitis, poisoning or trauma) or slowly developing (chronic hepatitis, cirrhosis or tumours).

◆ **SIGNS OF DISEASE**
These vary widely, from liver swelling or shrinkage, jaundice (yellowing), fluid accumulation in the abdomen, weight loss and changes in the colour of the faeces, to effects on the nervous system.

◆ **DIAGNOSIS**
Veterinary investigation will generally involve blood tests, X-rays or ultrasound examination, taking a urine sample or a liver biopsy.

◆ **TREATMENT**
This is mainly through careful control of the dog's diet and medication.

SKIN DISEASES

The skin is a layer of tissue that covers and protects the dog's body and collects sensory information about the external environment. Skin disease is very common in dogs, and may affect all areas, including the feet, ears, and any skin folds.

◆ Signs of Disease

These are commonly seen as itching, scratching, redness, discharges from the skin surface, skin thickening, scaling, change in hair colour or hair loss.

◆ Causes

The causes are numerous, but include:

◆ Parasites (fleas, ticks, mites, lice).

◆ Allergies to parasites, inhaled dust and pollens, food or chemical products.

◆ Bacterial, viral or fungal infections.

◆ Hormonal imbalances, poor diet, immune disorders.

◆ Skin warts, tumours, blocked anal glands and wax-filled ears may all cause local distress and lead to self trauma and local infection.

◆ Diagnosis

Your vet will probably ask you numerous

STRUCTURE OF THE SKIN

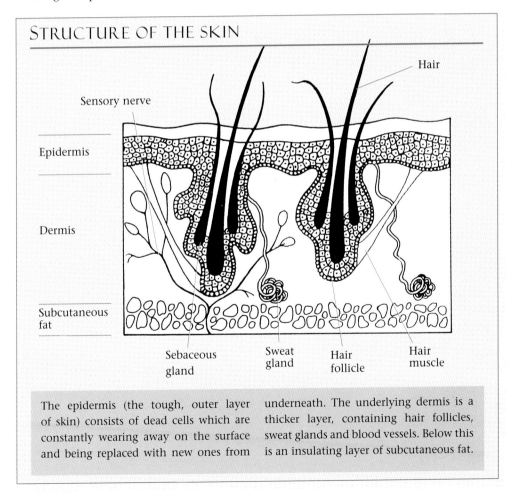

Sensory nerve

Epidermis

Dermis

Subcutaneous fat

Hair

Sebaceous gland

Sweat gland

Hair follicle

Hair muscle

The epidermis (the tough, outer layer of skin) consists of dead cells which are constantly wearing away on the surface and being replaced with new ones from underneath. The underlying dermis is a thicker layer, containing hair follicles, sweat glands and blood vessels. Below this is an insulating layer of subcutaneous fat.

questions about your dog's history, lifestyle, contacts and diet, and in a more complex case may need to take samples of coat brushings, skin scrapings, blood samples and bacteriological swabs.

◆ TREATMENT

The aim is to eliminate the cause of disease. Persistent cases, particularly those involving allergies, may need long-term treatment with steroid drugs.

EAR DISEASE

The ears are made up of four main parts: the outer flap, the external canal (down to the eardrum), the middle ear and inner ear (hearing and balance). The common ear diseases are mostly due to infection with bacteria, yeasts or ear mites, the presence of foreign bodies, such as grass seeds, or excess hair and wax. The lining of the ear canal is skin, so any disease affecting the skin can also affect the ear canal itself.

◆ SIGNS OF DISEASE

These include head shaking, scratching, a smell or discharge from the ear and pain.

◆ DIAGNOSIS

An otoscope is used to look down into the ear (this might be painful if the ear is very inflamed) and swabs may be taken for analysis when there is infection.

◆ TREATMENT

This is to clear the accumulated discharge and eliminate the infection, but in severe

GRASS SEED IN THE EAR

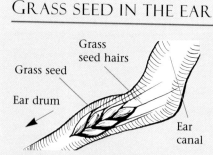

After becoming trapped on the underside of the outer ear flap (pinna), a grass seed can work its way down the ear canal towards the ear drum. Its hairs prevent it from travelling back up the ear canal. Prompt veterinary treatment is required to avoid serious infection.

cases may involve surgery to improve the air circulation to the ear canal, or to remove chronically infected tissue.

Note: repeated scratching and shaking of the head can damage the blood vessels in the ear flap, leading to the formation of a large blood blister, an aural haematoma, in the ear flap. This will need surgical drainage. Consult your vet.

EYE DISEASE

Whereas pedigree dogs are susceptible to a wide range of inherited structural eye diseases, the problems affecting mongrels are more due to infection and injury.

◆ SIGNS OF EYE DISEASE

These include a discharge (clear or pus),

squinting (eye half closed), rubbing at the eye, or protrusion of the third eyelid. Trauma to the transparent cornea on the front of the eye may lead to a corneal ulcer, which is painful for the dog and, if untreated, may progress to a ruptured eye.

◆ **Conjunctivitis** is inflammation of the tissues around the eye, commonly due to bacterial infection.

◆ **Cataracts** As the lens ages, or as a result of diseases such as diabetes, it may become increasingly opaque, with the dog's vision deteriorating. In severe cases, the lens may dislocate from its normal position; surgery may be possible to remove a cataractous lens.

◆ **Trauma** Severe trauma, for example, after a road accident, may force the eye out of its socket. Damage to the cornea may include punctures or tears. Both these conditions need urgent veterinary attention (see First Aid, page 121).

URINARY SYSTEM DISEASE

Circulating blood passes through the kidneys, which filter out waste products and excess water. The urine produced passes down the ureters to the bladder, where it is stored until being passed via the urethra to the exterior. Kidney failure leads to the build up of waste products in the bloodstream.

◆ **SIGNS OF DISEASE**
Kidney disease in a dog may cause the accumulation of waste products in the

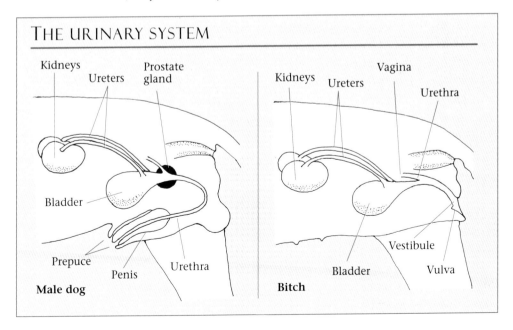

THE URINARY SYSTEM

Kidneys
Ureters
Prostate gland

Bladder

Prepuce
Penis
Urethra
Male dog

Kidneys
Ureters
Vagina
Urethra

Vestibule
Bladder
Vulva
Bitch

body (uraemia), due to an inability to filter blood, whereas bladder diseases may show up as an increased frequency of urination, pain on urination or the presence of blood or pus in the urine. Abnormally high levels of various salts in the urine can lead to the formation of crystals and stones; these may eventually cause a urinary blockage. Urinary obstruction is painful and distressing. It is most common in male dogs. If your dog repeatedly tries to pass urine but cannot, see your vet. Cystitis is common in bitches – when they strain to pass urine, a few drops are passed. Laboratory analysis of urine and blood samples will be part of the normal investigation.

Dogs may also suffer from incontinence, due to immaturity, nerve injury or old age; some of these cases are now treatable. You should visit your vet if your dog has any significant changes in his normal pattern of drinking or urination.

REPRODUCTIVE ORGANS

The testes in the scrotum produce sperm for the male dog, and the ovaries in the bitch's abdomen produce eggs. Normal mating involves the introduction of sperm into the female vagina via the penis. In the bitch, the muscles of the vagina contract towards the end of mating, retaining the penis in the vagina, and leading to what is called a 'tie'.

THE REPRODUCTIVE SYSTEM

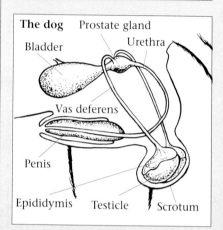

Sperm and testosterone are produced in the male dog's testicles. Sperm pass into the epididymis for storage, thence via the vas deferens during mating.

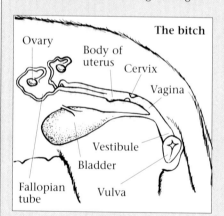

Eggs are produced in the ovaries and enter the uterus through the fallopian tubes. During the heat period, they can be fertilized by sperm.

◆ It is not unusual for a male dog to have a discharge from the sheath, but if associated with repeated licking, a heavy discharge or noticeable smell, there may be infection present. Unequal swellings in the testicles may be due to infection or tumours. Enlargement of the prostate gland may cause difficulty urinating.

◆ Signs of a pyometra in a bitch include an increase in thirst, a reduction in appetite, lethargy and a purulent vaginal discharge, typically around one month after a season.

◆ **FALSE PREGNANCY**

After a normal season, some dogs will show signs of a false pregnancy, e.g. behaviour changes, milk production, bed making, carrying shoes or other small objects around the house. The dog hormonally 'thinks' that she is pregnant, despite not having been mated. These signs mostly pass off without treatment, but are another good argument for spaying. Inflammation and infection of the mammary glands are called mastitis, and warrants veterinary attention.

NERVOUS SYSTEM DISEASE

Sensory information from internal and external sense organs, such as the ears, eyes and nose, is sent along the nerves to the central nervous system in the dog's spinal cord and brain, which are heavily protected by the skull and the spine. However, the nervous system is very susceptible to injury, whether from blunt trauma (e.g. road accidents), infection (e.g. canine distemper) or poisoning.

◆ **SIGNS OF NERVOUS SYSTEM DISEASE**

These are varied and include dullness or depression, pain, increased excitability, twitching or full-blown convulsions. All changes in the state of consciousness of your dog will warrant a full veterinary examination (see First Aid, Convulsions page 120).

THE SKELETAL SYSTEM

This is made up of the bones, muscles and joints. Bones have a calcified protein structure, and are strong but brittle; hence they break fairly easily. At the joints, the ends of the bones are covered with a low-friction, smooth cartilage surface and encased in a sac of sticky fluid – joint fluid – to lubricate them. A system of muscles is attached to the skeleton so as to move the limbs as required.

◆ **ARTHRITIS**

This is a degenerative inflammation of the joints, commonly in response to age, trauma or infection. The signs are of pain, lameness and joint swelling. Treatment depends on the cause, but often involves the long-term use of anti-inflammatory drugs (see First Aid, Fractures, page 117, Dislocation, page 120).

THE SKELETON

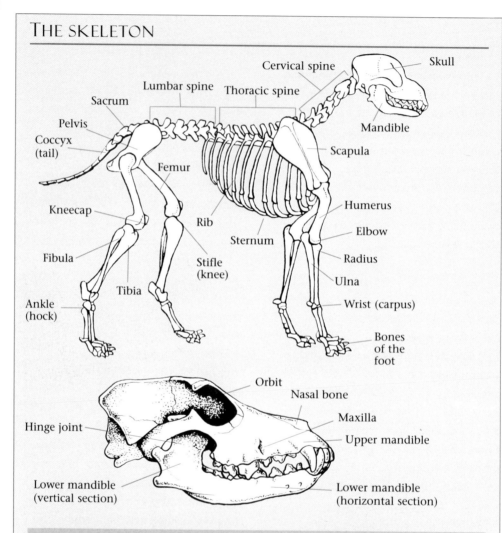

Cervical spine

Skull

Lumbar spine   Thoracic spine

Sacrum

Pelvis

Mandible

Coccyx
(tail)

Scapula

Femur

Kneecap

Humerus

Rib

Elbow

Sternum

Fibula

Radius

Stifle
(knee)

Ulna

Tibia

Ankle
(hock)

Wrist (carpus)

Bones
of the
foot

Orbit

Nasal bone

Hinge joint

Maxilla

Upper mandible

Lower mandible
(vertical section)

Lower mandible
(horizontal section)

The skeleton is the framework for the body. All the dog's ligaments, muscles and tendons are attached to the bones, 319 of them in total. By a process called ossification, cartilage template is calcified to produce bone. Bones are living tissue and they respond to the stresses and strains placed upon them. To build and keep healthy bones, dogs need a nutritionally balanced diet which contains an adequate supply of calcium, vitamin D and phosphorus.

FIRST AID AND EMERGENCIES

The main aim of first aid is to provide emergency care and treatment of a sick or injured animal before full veterinary treatment can be arranged. Genuine emergencies include collapse, major injuries or bleeding, prolonged epileptic fits, severe diarrhoea and vomiting blood, difficulty in breathing, prolonged whelping, burns and poisoning. Some of these are covered below.

BLEEDING

◆ The escape of blood from a damaged blood vessel is called haemorrhage. Clean away any obvious dirt, and apply a clean pressure dressing, to protect the wound from further contamination and to slow the blood flow. A sterile non-adherent dressing, such as melanin, some cotton wool and a new conforming bandage, is ideal, but, failing that, improvise with a clean handkerchief and a long strip of cloth. If blood soaks through the first

layer, apply another on top – don't keep opening it up to check!

BROKEN BONES (FRACTURES)

◆ Bone fractures are always painful, but it can be very difficult to assess their severity at home. All cases of sudden onset lameness, especially after an obvious accident, should be examined

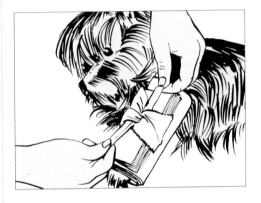

promptly by your vet, so call straight away for advice. Small cracks in young bones (greenstick fractures) may need no more than a support dressing and a couple of weeks' strict rest, whereas a major fracture involving a joint and with skin and muscle injuries may threaten the dog's ability to use the leg again.
◆ If your dog can walk on the other three legs, and there is no serious bleeding, it is generally better to restrict movement rather than try to apply

dressings and carry him. If he cannot walk, this may be due to shock, multiple fractures or a back (spinal) injury, so improvise a stretcher (see page 122).

◆ Where the injury is in the lower leg, and there is a lot of movement and pain, keep your dog still by reassuring him until you can see the vet. Generally, dressings do not help much and half-applied dressings that slip down may make matters worse.

◆ The only time when it is important to apply a dressing is when there is an open wound (see Bleeding, page 117 and Wounds, page 126).

BURNS

◆ These are where the body tissues are damaged by heat, chemicals, electricity (including lightning) or radiation (e.g. sunburn). With electrical injuries always turn off the supply at the main switch. Where the outer layer of skin is lost, there may be extensive fluid loss and infection. Burns need to be cleaned and kept sterile with regular dressings and antibiotics. Burns from house fires tend to be complicated by smoke damage to lungs and eyes. Use cold water to reduce the temperature of simple burns.

CHOKING

◆ Many dogs love playing with balls and other small objects that they can carry in their mouths, but do not use any that are

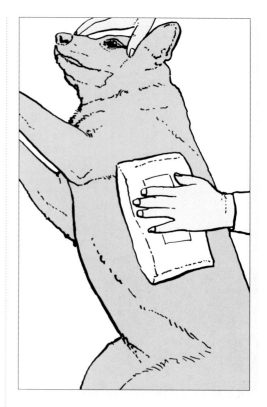

small enough to go into the dog's throat. A ball half swallowed by mistake can block the passage of air and instantly cause a life-threatening choke.

◆ If this happens, move fast – your dog cannot breathe. If you cannot restrain your dog and reach the obstruction with a pair of pliers or tongs, try short, sharp, hard pushes to the abdomen, upwards and forwards, just below the ribcage (called the Heimlich manoeuvre in people). This is more likely to be effective than trying to dislodge the object from the throat with your fingers.

THE ABC OF FIRST AID

The golden **ABC** for a collapsed animal is:
◆ **Airway** – is there anything blocking the airway through the mouth or throat, such as food or vomit, a ball or a bone? Be very careful if you have to put your fingers into the mouth: far better to use a piece of wood between the teeth to hold the mouth open than risk being bitten by a dog who is not fully aware of what he is doing.

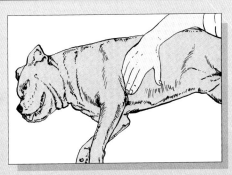

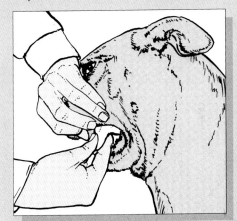

◆ **Breathing** – is the animal's chest rising and falling? The normal breathing rate for a dog is between ten and thirty breaths per minute, or one every two to six seconds. If he is not breathing, gently compress the broadest part of the chest once every two seconds. Alternatively, holding the mouth closed, breathe into the nostrils to inflate the lungs repeating every two to three seconds.
◆ **Circulation** – can you feel a heart beat? Feel or listen to the side of the chest just behind the left elbow. A normal pulse rate for a dog is between

seventy and 150 beats per minute, or one to two beats per second. If there is no heart beat, try cardiac massage: with the dog on his side, firmly squeeze the lower part of the chest just behind the elbows, once a second. Every fourth beat, gently compress the whole chest wall.
Note: call your vet, and go straight to the veterinary clinic.

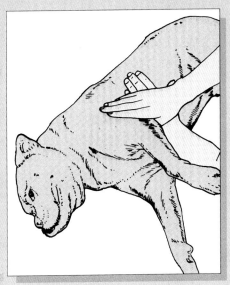

COLLAPSE

◆ A dog is collapsed when he is either suddenly or gradually unable to stand or coordinate his movements. It may be due to a wide range of causes, such as severe heart disease, serious injury, choke, internal bleeding, a metabolic problem, heatstroke, acute back pain, fits or poisoning. Treat as an emergency and contact your vet.

CONVULSIONS

◆ A dog may be having a fit if there are muscle tremors and twitching or violent muscle spasms. These may be accompanied by frothing at the mouth and the passing of urine and faeces. The fit may be caused by epilepsy, poisoning, a metabolic disorder (e.g. low blood levels of glucose or calcium), infection or injury to the nervous system.

◆ A classic epileptic fit will last just two to three minutes, although at the time this may seem much longer. It is not in itself an emergency. Your dog is best left well alone: clear away any fragile items or electrical cables, dim the lights and keep the noise levels down. It is rare for a dog to swallow his tongue, so keep your fingers away from his mouth to avoid being bitten. As the convulsions subside, the dog will regain consciousness, although he may seem dazed and confused for a while afterwards. Arrange for him to have a full veterinary check-up.

Note: if the dog does not come out of the fit in a few minutes, you should contact your vet and arrange to take him to the clinic straight away.

DIARRHOEA

◆ A dog who is vomiting and is passing quantities of blood-stained diarrhoea has a haemorrhagic gastroenteritis. This may be caused by a virus, such as parvovirus, or one of a number of bacterial infections. He may rapidly become dehydrated and may go into shock from fluid loss.

◆ Do not give anything further by mouth, and seek veterinary help as soon as possible, as your dog may need to go on an intravenous drip to save his life.

◆ Simple diarrhoea without vomiting is best managed at home by going without food for twenty-four hours, and offering plenty of clean water to drink.

◆ Severe diarrhoea cases should receive veterinary care and will be better helped by drinking either a veterinary or a children's oral rehydration fluid (available from the chemist).

DISLOCATION

◆ A displacement of a bone from its proper position in a joint is called a dislocation. Unless there is a congenital deformity (which is rare in mongrels), a dislocation will only occur when there has been significant trauma.

◆ Common sites in the dog are the hip and the elbow. They are associated with loss of movement, pain and swelling.

Dislocations are better left without dressings. These injuries should be seen quickly: the faster they are replaced, the better the end result.

DROWNING

◆ Inhalation of water into the lungs, normally whilst swimming, may lead to your dog being unable to breathe and losing consciousness.
◆ Hold the dog up by his hind legs to clear excess fluid from the lungs and perform the resuscitation technique (see Collapse, page 120).

ELECTROCUTION

◆ The passage of electric current through the body may cause signs from mild irritation through to unconsciousness and cardiac arrest.
◆ For the latter, perform the resuscitation procedure (see Collapse, page 120) but always turn the electricity supply off at the mains first. Lightning strike is often accompanied by burns at the point of contact with the ground, pulmonary edema and paralysis. Chewing at electrical wires will cause burns to the mouth and lips.

EYE PROLAPSE

◆ A major injury to the head after, for example, a road traffic accident, may cause the eyeball to be forced out of the socket.
◆ Try to prevent the eye becoming soiled with dirt or hair, and take your dog straight to the vet. These eyes rarely function properly again, but if replaced quickly, give a reasonable cosmetic result.

FOREIGN BODY

◆ Any foreign material that causes a problem is termed a foreign body.
TYPICALLY THESE ARE:
◆ **Grass seeds in ears:** these are very irritating, with persistent head shaking and scratching. They need to be removed by your vet, possibly under anaesthesia.
◆ **Grass seeds in eyes:** discharge, pain, squinting, swelling. Check with the vet.
◆ **Grass seeds in the foot:** typically in mid-summer, affecting dogs with longer hair around their feet. Swelling and pain occur between the toes, forming an abscess. When this bursts, the seed may come out with the pus, or may need to be removed by your vet. Bathe the foot three times daily with warm salt water.
◆ **Wood splinter or grit in the eye:** copious rinsing with clean water may be enough to clear it, but foreign matter may be hidden behind the third eyelid, or embedded in the cornea. If pain persists, seek veterinary help.
◆ **Balls, bones, stones, small toys and lengths of string in the gut:** when inadvertently swallowed, all these items may cause an obstruction of the intestine, which can be very serious, causing persistent vomiting, pain and depression. Seek veterinary help.

◆ **Wood, bone or plant material in the mouth:** these items may become wedged between the teeth, causing distress and discomfort for the dog and, if left, local infection.

◆ **Dogs that have sticks thrown for them to chase,** do occasionally run onto those sticks, causing deep wounds to the chest or back of the mouth. Even though the main piece of wood is easily removed, splinters may remain in the depth of a wound, causing serious infection.

GASTRIC DILATION/TORSION

◆ **Gastric dilation/torsion complex** is where the stomach of the dog becomes inflated with air and then twists on its attachments within the abdomen, with disastrous consequences. It is one of the few genuine emergencies. Luckily, it is relatively rare, and typically affects larger, deep-chested dogs.

◆ A dog developing this problem will show sudden onset restlessness, dribbling of saliva, retching, pain and sometimes extreme swelling of the abdomen. This may rapidly deteriorate to shock and collapse, and needs very urgent veterinary attention to release the build up of gas, and restore normal blood circulation to the whole body.

HEART DISEASE

See the previous section (Heart and Circulation Diseases, page 107).

HEAT STROKE

◆ Dogs have thick fur coats on all the time, and can only cool off by panting and finding a cool corner or cold floor to lie on. Where the ambient temperature is high, such as in a hot car or on a very warm day, their cooling mechanisms may not be able to cope, and then their body temperature can start to rise, often with disastrous consequences. Dogs with heat stroke will be in great distress, panting heavily; their rectal temperature may rise to over 41°C (108°F), progressing through collapse to coma and death.

◆ They need cooling down rapidly: use buckets of cold water or a hose, and transport the dog to the veterinary clinic if response is not rapid.

◆ Prevention is better and easier than cure: never leave your dog in a car on a warm day.

INJURY

◆ The common serious injuries for dogs are road traffic accidents: these may vary from no more than a bump and a fright to serious multiple trauma.

◆ Is he conscious? Check your ABC (see page 119). Is he bleeding? Can he walk? Is he getting better or worse?

◆ If he panics, gently restrain him – don't get bitten – and put on his collar and lead. Use a belt if nothing else is available.

◆ If he cannot walk it is best to keep him immobile until the vet can attend. If you need to move him, put a muzzle

TEMPORARY MUZZLE

This will allow a nervous, distressed or injured dog to be examined safely, without the risk of being bitten. A tape or bandage is secured around the muzzle as illustrated. However, a muzzle should not be applied in the following circumstances:
■ Airway obstruction
■ Loss of consciousness
■ Compromised breathing or severe chest injury
1 Tie a knot in the bandage.
2 Wrap around the dog's muzzle with the knot under the lower jaw and tie on top of the muzzle.
3 Cross the ends under the jaw and tie firmly behind the dog's head.

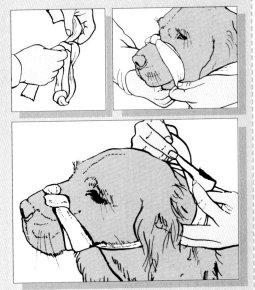

on him, improvise a stretcher with planks of wood, an old door or a blanket, and slide rather than lift him on to it. If he has injured his back, moving him very carefully may make the difference between walking again and permanent paralysis.
◆ Do not offer anything to eat or drink until he has been examined by the vet.

MILK FEVER
◆ Bitches producing large quantities of milk to feed a litter of puppies may run short of calcium in their circulating blood, with serious consequences.
◆ The signs include hypersensitivity,

tremors and twitching. Urgent treatment with intravenous calcium is essential.

PAIN
◆ Pain in dogs is usually associated with skeletal injury or trauma, back problems, cancers, abdominal disease, such as pancreatitis or peritonitis, or the passage of urinary stones.
◆ Sudden onset of acute pain, with yelping or whimpering and reluctance to move, may be due to back pain – for example, from a prolapsed intervertebral disc. Strict confinement of the dog is the best action until a full veterinary examination can be carried out.

POISONING

◆ A poison is anything that, when eaten, breathed in or absorbed through the skin, causes damage to the animal. Signs of poisoning are very variable, depending on the substance involved. The general advice given to dog owners is to:

◆ Prevent any further intake of poison.

COMMON POISONS

◆ **Antifreeze:** dogs like the taste, but it can cause convultions, coma, and death. You should provoke vomiting, and seek veterinary help.

◆ **Overdose with parasite treatment:** this is the result of over-enthusiastic owner dosing, causing twitching, salivating and frequent urination. If from external treatments, wash the coat to prevent any further absorption. Seek veterinary help.

◆ **Rat or mouse bait:** either dogs like the taste, or they may have eaten a poisioned rodent. Induce vomiting and take your dog to the vet.

◆ **Slug bait:** dogs like the taste. This can cause twitching, salivation, convulsions and coma. You should induce vomiting and go to the vet if any signs develop.

◆ **Chemicals:** spillages and accidents. Wash any traces from the skin and then contact your vet.

◆ **Prescription drugs:** contact your vet immediately.

◆ **Illegal drugs:** contact your vet.

◆ Keep a sample of the poison or the packet to show the vet.

◆ If the poison is recently ingested, you can stimulate vomiting by putting a pea-sized washing soda crystal on the back of your dog's tongue, or by making him drink a concentrated salt solution (one 5 ml teaspoon to a cup of water). However, some corrosive poisons can cause damage to the linings of the dog's throat and vomiting should only be induced after taking veterinary advice if the poisoning involves chemicals.

◆ Keep a sample of the vomit for analysis if necessary.

◆ Poisons on the coat should be washed off with a mild shampoo and then rinsed thoroughly with water.

SHOCK

◆ Shock is a very specific medical term for when there is sudden circulatory failure, due either to a major loss of blood or loss of the body's control over the heart and circulation.

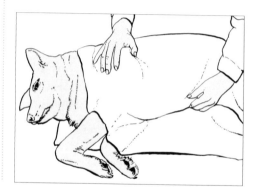

WHELPING

◆ **Pregnancy** in dogs lasts from fifty-seven to seventy-two days (an average of sixty-three days). Whelping is the process of the bitch giving birth to a litter of puppies, and it happens in three main stages.
◆ **Stage 1** is the start of the rhythmical contractions of the womb, normally lasting six to twelve hours.
◆ **Stage 2** involves the rhythmical contractions of the abdomen. It leads to the breaking of the waters, and results in the birth of puppies. The delay between each pup is variable: from five minutes to several hours, but if it is more than one hour, you should call your vet for advice.
◆ **Stage 3** is when the bitch passes the afterbirths, or placenta. It is common and normal for her to eat the placenta. In most mongrels whelping is trouble free.
◆ **Dystocia** is where she is unable to pass the pups normally, either because they are too big (large father/small mum), because of a previous injury to the bitch's pelvis, or because her metabolism will not let her go into the second stage of labour, e.g. lack of calcium in the blood. A true dystocia may mean that a caesarean will be necessary to deliver the pups.

◆ The signs are weakness or collapse, pale lips and gums (mucus membranes), cold skin and a fast heart rate.
◆ Ensure that your dog can breathe easily and cover him with a blanket to keep him warm. An animal in shock must be seen by a vet as soon as possible.

SNAKE BITES

◆ Two small puncture wounds on a lower limb, in summer-time, in an area known for the presence of snakes should make you suspicious of a snake bite. Treatment is aimed at limiting the spread of venom until a suitable serum can be administered.
◆ Use ice packs and tight bandages, and stop your dog running around until you contact your vet. Tourniquets should only be applied where there is expert knowledge as they can cause a lot of damage. Call your vet for advice.

STINGS

◆ The common stings are from bees and wasps. These rarely need treatment, but

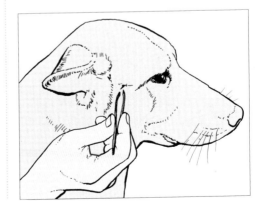

if causing much distress they can be soothed with cold water bathing or the use of an antihistamine cream.

◆ Try to remove a bee sting with some tweezers, but this may empty the rest of the bee venom into the wound, making things worse! If there is any swelling around the mouth or throat, call your vet.

◆ Some types of toad have toxins in their skin that can cause severe irritation, salivation and swelling to the mouth if picked up. Rinse the mouth well.

THIRST

◆ If you suspect that your dog has an increased thirst, start off by measuring the amount that he drinks each day. Anything over 100 ml (3½ fl oz) per 1 kg (2.2 lb) body weight is abnormal and should be investigated. Causes include diet, sugar diabetes, kidney and liver problems, pyometra, hormonal abnormalities, pain and fever. Call your vet.

VAGINAL DISCHARGE

◆ This may be due to a local vaginal infection or a pyometra. Consult your vet.

VOMITING

◆ Dogs vomit very easily. It protects them from the possible consequences of a fairly non-selective appetite, but repeated regular vomiting is abnormal.

◆ Withhold all food and water by mouth until the vomiting has stopped, then offer small amounts of water regularly. If the vomiting is persistent, seek veterinary help (see Diarrhoea, page 120).

WOUNDS

◆ **Large open wounds** need urgent veterinary attention. The main first aid objectives are to:

1 Prevent further injury.

2 Prevent contamination of the wound with dirt.

3 Control any bleeding.

◆ **Bite wounds** may be contaminated with bacteria from another dog's teeth, so need cleaning up as much as possible. Clip the hair from around the wound edges, and wash freely with clean water. Antibiotic treatment should be started quickly to limit any wound infection.

INDEX

USEFUL ADDRESSES

Royal Society for the
Prevention of
Cruelty to Animals
Causeway,
Horsham
West Sussex
RH12 1HG

Scottish Society for
the Prevention of
Cruelty to Animals
Braehead Mains
603 Queensferry Road
Edinburgh EH4 6EA

Ulster Society for the
Prevention of
Cruelty to Animals
11 Drumview Road
Lisburn
County Antrim
Northern Ireland
BT27 6YF

Irish Society for the
Prevention of
Cruelty to Animals
300 Lower Rathmines
Road
Dublin 6
Republic of Ireland

British Small Animal
Veterinary
Association
Kingsley House
Church Lane
Shurdington
Cheltenham
Glos
GL51 5TQ

British Veterinary
Association
7 Mansfield Street
London
W1M 0AT

Royal College of
Veterinary Surgeons
62-64 Horseferry Road
London SW1P 2AF

Blue Cross
1 Hugh Street
London SW1V 1QQ

Guide Dogs for
the Blind
Hillfields
Burghfield Common
Reading
Berks RG7 3YG

Hearing Dogs for
the Deaf
The Training Centre
London Road
Lewknor
Oxon
OX9 5RY

National Canine
Defence League
17 Wakley Street
London
EC1V 7LT

People's Dispensary
for Sick Animals
PDSA House
Whitechapel Way
Priorslee
Telford
Shropshire
TF2 9PQ

Wood Green Animal
Shelters
Highway Cottage
Chiswell Road
Heydon
Royston
Hertfordshire
SG8 8BR